ARCHAEOLOGY BENEATH THE SEA

George F. Bass

ARCHAEOLOGY BENEATH THE SEA

WALKER AND COMPANY • NEW YORK

First published in the United States of America in 1975
by the Walker Publishing Company, Inc.

Published simultaneously in Canada
by Fitzhenry & Whiteside, Limited, Toronto.

ISBN: 0–8027–0477–8

Dec. 2, 1975

Library of Congress Catalog Card Number: 74–24795

Printed in the United States of America.

10 9 8 7 6 5 4 3 2 1

To Ann

ACKNOWLEDGMENTS

Chapter IX first appeared, in nearly its present form, as "A Byzantine Trading Venture" in Scientific American *for August 1971; portions of chapters II and VII are taken from "A Bronze Age Shipwreck" and "The Museum Assembles a Fleet" in* Expedition, *the bulletin of the University Museum of the University of Pennsylvania, for Winter 1961 and Winter 1965 respectively, and parts of chapters X and XI are taken or adapted from "New Tools for Undersea Archaeology" in the* National Geographic *for September 1968. Much of chapter XIV first was published in the first number of the* Newsletter *of the American Institute of Nautical Archaeology in 1974, and a passage in chapter VI is taken from* National Geographic Society Research Reports, 1964. *The quotation from* Archaeology Under Water *in chapter VIII is reprinted by permission of Thames and Hudson Ltd.*

Harriet Maggi made the original drawings for the Prologue, as well as two maps, and Richard Schlecht drew the ship reconstructions in Chapter IX.

I wish to thank the photographers who provided illustrations, and the National Geographic Society, through its president, Melvin M. Payne, for permission to use many of its pictures of my work.

Peter Throckmorton, Yüksel Eğdemir, Eric Ryan, Susan Womer Katzev, David Leith, Ann Bass, Claude Duthuit, Donald Rosencrantz, J. Richard Steffy, and Frederick van Doorninck refreshed my memory by reading various stages of the manuscript, and David Grimland, Gay Piercy, and Robert D. Bass made helpful comments. To these friends I express my gratitude.

GFB

Contents

ARCHAEOLOGY BENEATH THE SEA

Prologue–1200 B.C.

~~~~~~~~~~~~~~~~~~~~~~~~~~~~~~~~~~~
~~~~~~~~~~~~~~~~~~~~~~~~~~~~~~~~~~~
~~~~~~~~~~~~~~~~~~~~~~~~~~~~~~~~~~~

THE great double-bladed bronze axe bit deeply into the wood. The voyager had risen at dawn to fell the tallest trees on the island; this was the twentieth and last to topple. He stripped branches from the trunks and, with a polished metal adze cut smooth planks to form a hull. With an auger he bored holes for wooden pegs to hold the planks fast.

Within four days the boat, wide as a broad-bottomed merchant-man, was finished. Decking was complete, and mast, yard, steering oar, and cloth sail were ready. He spread a layer of brushwood dunnage over the interior of the hull before hauling it down to the shore on rollers. With meat, a leather bag of grain, and skins holding wine and water, the sailor bade his beautiful helper good-bye and sailed out onto the wine-dark sea.

On the eighteenth day of his voyage, a canopy of lowering clouds blackened the sky. Confused winds whipped the sea into unruly hordes of whitecapped peaks. A mountainous wave shattered the tiny craft, tearing planks apart and scattering them like chaff. The sailor, first clinging to a single timber and then swimming alone, reached one more foreign shore. His adventures were not yet over.

The sailor, of course, was Odysseus, known also by his Latin

I

name Ulysses, most famous of all seafarers. The nymph Calypso had been ordered by none other than Zeus to help him return to his native island of Ithaca, but once more Poseidon blocked his way. It was the tenth year after the fall of Troy.

In this period another small ship sank to the bottom of the Mediterranean. No poet described her construction. Her captain was not a hero. But she was a real ship, not shrouded in the half-truths of mythology.

She had been built far to the east by an anonymous shipwright. He probably spoke a Semitic language rather than Greek, but he used exactly the same tools and techniques to form his small trading vessel, between thirty and thirty-five feet long, of cypress and oak. He, too, lined the inside with brushwood to protect the fragile planks.

About 1200 B.C., in the twilight of the Eastern Mediterranean Bronze Age, the little vessel made her last voyage. We do not know if she was involved in the events of her time. Perhaps her captain had heard of the battles at Troy, far up the Anatolian coast. Troy was only one of the trouble spots. Farther inland, the Hittite Empire was crumbling. Enigmatic warriors prepared a land and sea assault on Egypt to the south. The famed Greek citadels of Mycenae, Tiryns, and Pylos, homes of the Homeric heroes, were under attack by unknown enemies. Within the century a Dark Age would cast its shadow over Greece, ending literacy, monumental architecture, art, and the ease of communications that had stimulated creativity among Mycenaean craftsmen.

The ship probably sailed from a sandy shore in Syria. A single square sail, we suppose, carried her lightly over the waves toward Alasia, the island later called Cyprus after the rich deposits of copper mined in her mountains. On reaching the island the vessel hugged its coast, putting in at night wherever shelter could be found.

Away from the roll of the open sea, the captain carefully poured oil into the shallow clay lamp he had purchased earlier on the Syro-Palestinian coast. By its flickering light he inspected the items he hoped would make this a successful trading venture.

Around him, near the stern, lay his personal possessions: balance-pan weights for weighing trade goods, metalworking tools, a few scarabs as religious talismans, and a seal. The last was his official stamp, a pencil-slim cylinder of carved reddish stone to be rolled across wet clay documents and container sealings. Carved

THE EASTERN MEDITERRANEAN

centuries before in North Syria, it was probably an heirloom passed proudly from father to son.

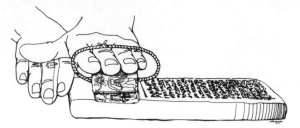

At least three of five scarabs, shaped like frozen white dung beetles with Egyptian hieroglyphs on their stomachs, were also antique. They, too, had been manufactured on the Asian coast, by a local craftsman who didn't even know proper Egyptian. Still, they had brought good luck so far and couldn't be taken lightly.

Provisions were stored in pottery containers of the types available in almost any Syrian or Cypriot marketplace. Half a dozen two-handled jars of red-brown clay, some as tall as a man's knee, held water or wine; three smaller jars, imitations of a popular Greek shape, probably held olive oil. There may have been sacks or bags of grain as well.

A crew member had earlier collected from the stern the brush-cutting tools he needed to prepare a small fire ashore. Meat, skewered on a slim bronze spit, now shed sizzling tears of fat into glowing coals. Steam rose from an ember-blackened cooking pot—perhaps from gruel of barley or wheat meal, which had been ground in a pair of stumpy-legged stone mortars brought from Syria.

Cypriot jugs of fair, sandy texture were filled and passed around the fire. The captain drank from the finest goblet, decorated with bands of red paint and tiny incised strokes cut into the leather-hard clay before it was fired.

Not many days out of home port, they reached the place where copper was traded, one of numerous Cypriot coastal towns that prospered from the metal traffic. Arguing and bickering with the local merchants over the quality of the goods they had to barter, they unloaded their cargo. What it was we do not know: jars of wine or oil, finely wrought metal vases, textiles, livestock, precious materials brought from voyages to other lands?

In return, thirty-four wide, flat, four-handled ingots were brought to the edge of the sea on the shoulders of harbor workers. The ore had been smelted far up in the hills, where the molten metal was cast in shallow molds cut into the earth. The handles made them easier to carry than the old-style ingots their grandfathers had traded.

Some of the ingots had been stamped with Cypriot signs while still liquid; others were marked with signs scratched into the congealed metal. Some of the marks probably assured the merchant that the copper was almost pure, but since no two ingots weighed just the same, he still had to check and record the weight of each. Today they would average about fifty-five pounds apiece, but he worked with the weight systems of his day.

Just as an international trader must now convert from pounds to kilograms, the merchant was prepared to weigh his wares according to the standards of the countries he visited. He owned sixty balance-pan weights of haematite, a hard stone the color of dried blood. They formed sets that could be used throughout the Eastern Mediterranean: Egyptian qedets, *Hebrew* shekels, *and Syrian* neṣefs. *Multiples and fractions, polished to a fine accuracy, came in a variety of shapes; most were either like pointed eggs (flattened on one side to prevent rolling), or like modern marshmallows, slightly swollen on their tops.*

The ingots were wrapped in matting so that they would not shift position when stacked in the hold of the ship. Around them the captain stowed fragments of ingots that had been cut into smaller pieces.

Already on board, most probably, was the other ingredient needed for making bronze: tin. Few men knew the source of the rare rectangular bars, which had been cast in some far-off land, and the captain was not about to divulge his secret.

It was more convenient to cast new bronze tools and weapons by simply melting down old bronzes than by mixing copper and tin together. The merchant was pleased to see that plenty of scrap was available. Bits and pieces of broken plow tips, picks, hoes, knives, axes, and adzes were brought by the basketful, weighed, and placed around the stacked ingots. Some of the scrap had already been melted into pancake-shaped pieces that were easier to work with. A few small, oblong bronze ingots were especially valuable for they had been cast to exactly the same weight and could be used almost as currency in an age before the invention of coinage; these the captain stacked with his personal belongings near the stern. There, too, he placed a folded sheet of tinfoil, thin as a leaf. Two lumps of unworked rock crystal, to be fashioned into beads or ornamental pinheads, completed the inventory of merchandise he kept separate; other trinkets—scores of glass beads and a bronze bracelet of adjustable size—he dropped into a small jar and left with the bulkier cargo.

Under way again, the captain made for a landfall on the southern coast of Asia Minor. He steered across a shoreless sea, the high mountains of Anatolia invisible through the haze ahead. Only on clear, crisp winter days were they sometimes to be seen from Cyprus, often capped with snow. But in winter, with winds too unpredictable for sailing, merchant ships were pulled up for hibernation on dry land.

He followed the usual route of Syrian seafarers bound westward from Cyprus. His exact destination is unknown: Rhodes, Crete, the Greek mainland, a town on the western edge of Asia Minor?

Whatever his ultimate port, the merchant-captain was well prepared to set up shop. In the center of his ship lay a flat, close-grained stone, far larger than the ballast stones below the cargo. Using it as an anvil, he could shape unworked bronze castings with the two round hammers which he kept close at hand; the socket for the wooden handle of one was lined with a thin copper sheathing to absorb some of the violence of the blows that might otherwise have cracked the stone head.

Once he had hammered a socket onto a metal tool, using his swage, and pounded thin the end of its blade on his anvil, the merchant sharpened it to a fine edge with the whetstone that dangled from his neck. He added a final, burnished luster with one of dozens of stone polishers stored near the stern.

Everything he needed for smithing could be found on board— except for furnaces, which were made quickly of stone and clay along the route. He carried a supply of clay, perhaps for molds.

When he reached the land we now call Turkey, he coasted west-
ward. Shipboard life was as routine as the sea permits among its
visitors. Crew members kept their vessel in good repair, mending
rents in the sail with a bronze needle, and cutting mortises to
replace damaged timbers with a wooden-handled bronze chisel
kept safely near their master's other tools. Sometimes they caught
fish, using lead-weighted lines and nets, to be cooked ashore; meals
at sea were cold. (Was it the helmsman who carelessly spit the pits
from a handful of olives into the dunnage near his feet?) Beards
were trimmed with a crescent-shaped razor as thin as the papyrus
sheets that Egyptian captains carried.

They safely crossed the Bay of Antalya, where at least one ingot-
carrying ship had gone down years before. Ahead lay Cape Gelido-
nya. There currents, suddenly and without warning, run as force-
fully as any in the Mediterranean.

The captain undoubtedly feared the cape—it was dreaded by
sailors throughout antiquity. Should he steer between the cape and

the row of tiny islands, which extend its line into the sea, or, giving the cape as wide a berth as possible, seek passage between the islands themselves?

Just as Homeric seamen prayed for a sign from the gods before deciding their course, he may have sought divine guidance from Yamm, his own sea god. Among his good-luck charms was a single astragal, the knucklebone from a sheep or goat. A toss of the bone, causing it to land on one of its four distinctive sides, would provide an omen.

He chose the islands. Trying to thread her way between them, perhaps drawn irresistibly by the current, the ship ran onto jagged rocks.

She sank straight down the almost vertical, submerged face of the island. Her stern caught on the cliff a few feet off the bottom, tilting her slightly to starboard, as her bows settled onto the seabed. Within a few years most of her timbers had been devoured by shipworms and her cargo of metal covered by a protective green patina. What was left would lie undisturbed for nearly 3,200 years.

CHAPTER I
A.D. 1960

"IF YOU don't grab the bull by the horns when you have the chance, you'll never get anywhere!"

I hurried timidly back to my student assistant's desk as Professor Rodney Young's deep voice followed me over the glass partition separating our offices. He had just asked me if I would be interested in directing an archaeological excavation in North Africa.

"I don't know Arabic," I'd answered. "And I don't know anything about surveying."

He suggested I might learn.

I had a dozen other excuses. But mainly I felt that I didn't remember very much about archaeology—or history, or Greek, or French, or German for that matter. In seminars facts stayed tantalizingly close to the tip of my tongue, but four years away from classes had pushed them too far back.

I had just come from two years in the army, the last spent in charge of an isolated platoon north of Uijongbu, Korea. I had become an excellent pool shot, was nearly as good at Ping-Pong, and had seen approximately four hundred different movies in four hundred consecutive evenings. And I had learned a lot about trucks and generators and water pumps and cesspools and kitchens. But none of this helped much in courses on Hellenistic Archaeology or Iron Age Greece. Before the army I had been at the American School of Classical Studies in Athens for two years, visiting museums and ruins, assisting on excavations in Greece and Turkey. All that, and my four years at the Johns Hopkins University were now only an imprecise memory as I began, in 1959, my first semester of graduate studies at the University of Pennsylvania.

Whether or not I wanted to go to Africa didn't matter in the end; by the time of our discussion, I learned, another director had already been chosen by the sponsors of the dig. But I remembered Rodney Young's advice.

A month later Dr. Young called me to his office to read a letter from John Huston, head of the Council of Underwater Archaeology in San Francisco. It was about ancient shipwrecks in the Mediterranean, and a Peter Throckmorton who had located dozens of them while living on a Turkish sponge boat. Throckmorton, a professional photo-journalist and skilled diver, felt that ships could be excavated under water as carefully as buried cities are uncovered on land. He wondered who might sponsor a scientific expedition to Turkey. Because of Dr. Young's excavations at Gordion, in Turkey, Huston had suggested the University of Pennsylvania Museum.

One of the wrecks, Throckmorton had told him, was from the Late Bronze Age. A ship from the time when Agamemnon quarreled with Achilles on the beach at Troy. A ship from the time when Odysseus set sail for home across the wine-dark sea. A ship more than three thousand years old.

"Would you want to learn how to dive to be the expedition archaeologist?" Young asked.

This time I grabbed for the bull's horns.

"Sure," I said. Without hesitation.

Peter Throckmorton and I first met in a hotel lobby in New York just after Christmas; he had come directly from Greece to the 1959 meeting of the Archaeological Institute of America. I was struck most by his intensity. He kept on his light topcoat as if always ready to leave. His strong face appeared closer than it really was, and he fixed a long, searching stare at me through horn-rimmed glasses.

Seated around a conference table that night, Dr. Young, John Huston, and I listened, with several others, to Peter's story. Unlike some people who are obsessed with an idea and talk faster and faster, Peter spoke slowly and deliberately, frequently punctuating his remarks with an "unh?" to be sure we were all still with him. Ash trays and cigarette packs formed islands and wrecks as he organized and dismantled maps of the areas where his most promising sites lay.

Over and over he stressed the urgency of an expedition:

"If we don't do it now, this year, sponge divers will dynamite the Bronze Age cargo for scrap metal. It can't wait past this summer."

A similar wreck had been found a generation earlier by Greek divers working Turkish waters, and hundreds of pounds of copper and bronze artifacts melted down and sold. Before we broke up that evening, we had agreed to form an expedition.

Peter and I went alone back to his Thirty-first Street loft and talked till dawn. He had sailed small boats in the Pacific, been in the Korean War, done professional salvage work, studied anthropology in Mexico and Paris, covered the Algerian revolution dressed as a rebel, gone on to India to shoot a tiger-hunt story for *Argosy,* and ended up in Bodrum, the sponge center of Turkey, to write a book about sponge divers and to investigate stories of ancient ships. I noticed a dusty top hat in the back of a closet shelf, and he laughed, embarrassed, mumbling something about his boyhood "society" days. Now he was dedicated to one thing: shipwrecks.

Peter had done everything I knew only from books. In high school and college I had read everything I could find on diving, but it never occurred to me that I might, myself, one day strap tanks on my back. My only experience with "underwater archaeology" was near Lerna, a prehistoric town in southern Greece where I received my first training in archaeological field work. There, naively expecting to find ancient vases like Easter eggs in the seaweed an arm's length below me, I swam along the shore wearing my first mask, its plastic faceplate so badly scratched it was more translucent than transparent, a pair of rubber duck-feet, and a snorkel with Ping-Pong-ball float trapped in its curved upper end.

Peter showed me an impressive volume, his log of two summers in Turkey. Charts and sketch plans and descriptions were accompanied by photographs and drawings: undisturbed cargoes of Roman and Byzantine wine jars protruding from the seabed; huge glass chunks of unknown date, all that remained of a ton of colored glass ingots salvaged by sponge divers; the veiled bronze head of a mournful lady, larger than life size, pulled from the sea in a sponge-dragger's net; terracotta lamps and jugs of different periods of Classical antiquity; and then there was the material from Cape Gelidonya.

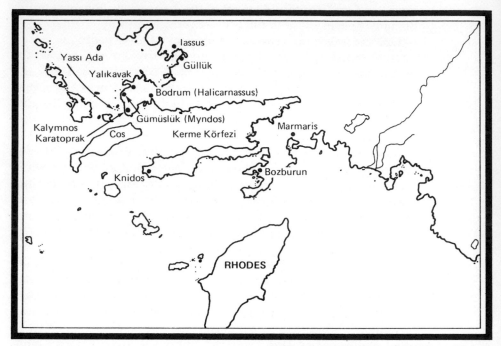

THE SOUTHWEST TURKISH COAST

In 1958, Peter said, he had met Captain Kemal Aras, a leading Bodrum sponge diver, who showed him many wrecks and told him of more. One of those that Peter only heard about lay between two small islands just off Cape Gelidonya, the western tip of the Bay of Antalya in southwest Turkey. About a hundred feet deep, Kemal said, he had found corroded bronze implements. Their description piqued Peter's curiosity more than anything else he had heard. But it was not until a year later, acting as guide to a diving expedition headed by Drayton Cochran, that he was able to reach the spot and dive on it. In a few days the group raised sufficient samples from the site to offer proof of its date: the Late Bronze Age, between 1600 and 1100 B.C.

There were bronze picks, double-bladed axes, a rapier like spit, a hoe blade and a knife blade, and curious, flat four-handled ingots of copper, each about a foot wide and two feet long. Peter pulled out the reproduction of an Egyptian tomb-painting showing a man from Keftiu, the Egyptian name for Crete, bearing a similar ingot on his shoulder as tribute to the pharaoh. The few pottery fragments, alone, several of distinctive Mycenaean shape, were enough to date the collection to the time of Homer's heroes.

Did these pieces represent only part of an entire cargo on the sea floor, or were they all that had been there, just scraps of jetsam? Some of the potential expedition sponsors Peter approached suggested the latter. Peter remained convinced that it was a complete shipwreck, but he said he couldn't honestly be sure.

More all-night sessions followed. We ran up huge phone bills between New York and Philadelphia. A number of ancient wrecks in the Mediterranean had been partially salvaged or excavated, but never before had a shipwreck been excavated in its entirety, and never to the same exacting standards that are normal on land sites. How would we go about the job? What would we need? How much would it cost? How would we get it to Turkey?

Peter did most of the organizing, visiting manufacturers of diving and photographic equipment, getting reductions on prices, loans, and even outright gifts where possible. The University Museum agreed to provide most of the money we needed. Nixon Griffis, then president of Brentano's bookstores, and Harry Starr, president of the Littauer Foundation, promised additional support after watching slides in Peter's flat. Joan du Plat Taylor, of London University's Institute of Archaeology, wrote that she could bring equipment and funds from England.

There remained just one more river to cross. I still did not know how to dive.

I joined the Depth Chargers diving club at the Central Philadelphia YMCA. Our course was ten weeks long, but I had only six weeks left. In the sixth lesson we were still practicing with masks and snorkels in the pool and learning diving theory. I had yet to see an aqualung.

"Can I just try a tank on once, please?" I begged Dave Stith, the instructor. "I'm going to be working in about a hundred feet of water all summer."

A tank was strapped to my back. We went to the bottom of the pool and buddy-breathed its length and back sharing one mouthpiece. Then I took my final exam. Dave tossed the tank, weight-belt, mask, and fins onto the bottom at the deep end. I had to swim down, turn on the air, and put the whole thing on under water, something I had not yet done on dry land. Then he harassed me, pulling my mouthpiece out, turning off my air, and yanking the faceplate loose—sometimes, it seemed, all at once. I passed the test.

Peter and I worked through the night in the museum, packing and crating equipment for shipment. I slipped down to South Carolina for a weekend to get married. Ann returned to her studies at the Eastman School of Music. Peter and I left for Turkey.

Istanbul was filled that April with talk of revolution. An evening curfew confined us to our hotel night after night. There were riots against the government. A student was killed. It was the wrong time to get official business done. But crates of equipment were arriving by ship and train from America, France, Germany, and Greece. Peter and I trudged each day for a month through the same round of customs offices, drinking countless little cups of Turkish coffee, trying at first to work alone and then employing and discarding professional brokers. Nothing seemed to work.

We put the time to good use and piled our hotel room high with rope, cable, cotton waste, cooking pots, lead ingots, funnels, crowbars, sledge hammers, and all the other hardware we could buy in the markets. These were essentials. We had no funds for frivolous things—no camping equipment, not even a blanket for the entire expedition, much less tents. But soon we made friends in a nearby army surplus yard and hauled away discarded parachutes, ripped mattresses, broken tools, mosquito nets, an old road compressor, and a battered jeep station wagon. Our army training in scrounging suddenly seemed as important as any academic courses we had taken.

I had still dived with tanks only once, to a depth of ten feet in the YMCA pool. I wanted to try going deeper. Oktay Ercan, a young Istanbul diver, took me out on the Bosphorus to the diving barge of the Türk Balikadamlar Kulubu (Fishmen's Club). One of the members handed me his rubber suit to wear. I'd never before seen a wet suit, the form-fitting jacket and pants of neoprene rubber which holds an insulating layer of water, quickly warmed by a diver's body, close to his skin. As I tried to pull on the tight pants one entire side came up with my hand in a long, soundless tear. Diving suits are almost impossible to find even today in Turkey, and neoprene glue for mending them does not exist. The suit was brand-new. The owner told me not to worry. Someone found another for me.

Tanks, mask, and fins on, I followed Oktay down a ladder into the cold currents. He hung onto a rung while I checked to see if I had the right number of lead weights on my belt. Then he swam down a few feet ahead of me as I pulled myself down a rope. At ten feet the pain in my ears was intense. I couldn't force myself down another inch and returned to the surface. My new friends offered suggestions for clearing my Eustachian tubes. Yawn. Swallow. Pinch your nose and blow. Go down feet first. I tried again and again. The deepest I got was ten or twelve feet. Here I was in Turkey, to excavate a wreck a hundred feet deep, and I couldn't dive deeper than ten. Some underwater archaeologist! I carefully undid all the gear and went back to the hotel.

A few days later Claude Duthuit came diving with me. Claude was to be one of the mainstays of the diving team. A French friend from Peter's earlier work in Turkey, he had just arrived from Paris where he had been assembling suction pipes and mapping devices for the excavation. He had spent some of his school years, during the war, in America, and his English was perfect.

This time we waded in from a nearby beach. Claude told me not to worry about my ears, we'd just swim around in a few feet so that I could get used to the equipment. It was a totally new experience, diving outside a pool. I followed tiny fish and poked, rather nervously, at growing things on the sand. Most unforgettable was the sound of every breath being drawn through the regulator hose and expelled in a rush of bubbles somewhere above my neck. It was the "sound of diving," the one thing that breaks the silence of underwater scenes in films and television programs.

We swam just below a small boat and followed the rusty chain beneath us to its anchor. Claude knelt down in the sea grass and showed me his depth gauge. Thirty feet! I hadn't yawned or swallowed or pinched my nose. I hadn't even noticed. The barrier was broken. If I was at thirty feet, it meant that my ears had cleared. I could go to any depth.

We still needed an excavation permit, and we still needed a customs permit for our equipment. The ministers who had to sign the documents had more important things on their minds than archaeology. Peter and I frantically chased blind leads back and forth between Istanbul and Ankara as the political situation worsened.

Finally good news came. The permit had been signed and mailed to us in Istanbul. It was time to celebrate.

The rumble of tanks on the street outside did not wake me from my first peaceful sleep in weeks. Nor did the marching soldiers who cordoned off the hotel to prevent anyone from leaving. In the lobby I heard that the revolution finally had come. The Menderes government was overthrown, and officials were fleeing the capital.

Oh, God. Our permit. Surely the officials who signed it were no longer in office. Would it be honored by the new regime? We waited and inquired until we could wait no longer. In despair we headed south, to Izmir, where the rest of the team Peter had recruited was assembling.

Honor Frost, a former draftsman for the British excavations at Jericho, who had dived with Peter around Bodrum, was to be in charge of making underwater plans. From Toulon came Frederic Dumas, chief diver; I recognized his face from scenes in Cousteau's *Silent World.* Nearing fifty, he was still considered by many to be the greatest diver in the world. Joan du Plat Taylor would not be diving, but would collaborate with me on the strictly archaeological work; she had directed excavations in Cyprus and the Near East, and was one of the first archaeologists to realize the full potential of underwater work. Herb Greer, expedition photographer who had not yet arrived, was driving down from London by motor scooter, busking en route with folk singer Rambling Jack Eliot. He was bearded, his head shaved, and he wrote plays, poetry and music. He had been a companion of Peter in Algeria. Claude, who had stayed behind to accompany some of the equipment in a truck, rounded out the team. We met together for the first time at the home of Mustafa Kapkin in Izmir, ancient Smyrna, a major harbor of the eastern Aegean, and Mustafa's photography studio still remains our unofficial office in Turkey.

It was a good group. Of that I was glad. But I was in an awkward position. Excavation permits are issued to institutions, not to individuals, and ours was to be in the name of the University Museum of the University of Pennsylvania; as the only representative of the museum in the group, I was officially the director. Not only was I, at twenty-seven, the youngest member, but I was the only inexperienced diver (except for Herb, who at least had finished his course), I knew no Turkish, and I would be working with a distinguished archaeologist who had been digging and publishing since I was born. Now the digging and publishing were my responsibility. I had much to learn.

Peter had done all of the work of organization, had picked the other staff members, and was the guiding spirit for the whole program; these were really his wrecks.

Bodrum was also Peter's. When we arrived from Izmir, a hundred hands must have been shoved through the station-wagon window to grasp his; had Bodrum been New York, it would have been a ticker-tape parade.

Bodrum has changed in the fourteen years since our group first straggled in. Now only four hours by paved road from Izmir, it is a major resort with hotels, pensions, garden restaurants, and discotheques. Our first summer there we met one tourist, a dusty German hitchhiker; today the main square is jammed with cars bearing Turkish and foreign license plates. And the quay, once the gathering place for the sponge fleets and fishing boats, is today mostly reserved for foreign yachts and tourist boats.

Only the first glimpse of Bodrum from the road remains unchanged. High above the town, after a long series of mountain curves, all looking alike, one sees suddenly the blue of the perfect harbor and the sea beyond, the dark green of trees, the red of tiled roofs, and the white of cubelike houses, domed cisterns, and sharp minarets pointing up at the cloudless blue sky. On either side are brown, barren hills, but straight ahead, like a protective barrier in the sea, is the long, dark ridge of Kara Ada, Black Island, and still farther away the blue-grey outline of the Greek island, Cos.

Dominating everything is the majestic fifteenth-century castle of St. Peter, its two central towers rising high above the town. From these towers, on a still day, you can see clearly the straight stone walls of the ancient harbor now below water level inside the modern harbor; the history of Bodrum as a major port goes back unknown centuries.

Just how early Bodrum was settled is not known. Its ancient name, Halicarnassus, suggests a distant time before the arrival of Greeks and the Greek language in the Aegean about 2000 B.C.; burials from the third millennium were recently found not far away. Mycenaean colonists, speaking an early form of Greek, arrived in the vicinity during the second millennium B.C., but are known only

The first view of Halicarnassus, modern Bodrum, from the Izmir road. The Crusader castle is built partly of blocks stolen from the ancient city.

from a Late Bronze Age cemetery several miles from Bodrum.

Classical Halicarnassus is well known. Herodotus the historian was born there. Its Queen Artemisia joined in the Battle of Salamis on the Persian side. The tomb for its King Mausolus was known as one of the Seven Wonders of the World, and left to us our own word for any sumptuous tomb; most of the sculptured frieze from the Mausoleum was taken to the British Museum in the mid-nineteenth century—long before strict antiquities laws—but fragments still turn up from time to time, used as building blocks in the fifteenth-century castle.

Sacked by Alexander the Great in 334 B.C., Halicarnassus declined in prestige and passed between Greek, Roman, Byzantine, Turkish, and Crusader hands, still retaining at the beginning of this century a strong mixture of Greeks and Turks. Now it is completely Turkish.

The hot, airless hotel in Bodrum was almost full, so Peter and I ended up in cots on the roof. The sound of donkeys and camel bells from the marketplace below, the buzz of flies, and a blinding, baking sun beating on our faces forced us out of bed not long after dawn. I joined Peter in two double-sized glasses of strong, hot tea, not knowing that before the day was over I would have drunk a glass of tea with the mayor, the director of schools, the harbor master, the owner of the sweet shop, countless sponge divers, the owner of the *hamam* (Turkish bath), and a young barber who plastered the walls of his modest shop with pictures of skin divers and thought that meeting Frederic Dumas was the high point of his life.

I was eager to see the finds from the wrecks, and Peter led me to the small museum he had started in the castle. We crossed the moat, climbed massive flights of stairs, passed a vaulted chapel, and arrived at the knights' dining hall. Inside, on a dirt floor lit only by small, high windows, were dozens of amphoras, large two-handled wine jars whose varied shapes offer clues to their dates and places of manufacture. Old Uncle Mehmet, castle watchman, carefully and proudly held up the pieces for me to examine. Each was labeled with the name of the boat captain or sponge diver who had donated it, when and where it had been found, and how deep. Peter excitedly described how the dining hall and chapel could be made into a unique museum, a center for underwater archaeology.

At night we sat on the waterfront, eating *köftes* and *dolmas* by the light of a dim lantern, drinking *raki* and talking to Captain Kemal Aras. Captain Kemal said he would work for us (Peter translated), bringing his sponge boat *Mandalinçi* and a crew of seasoned helmet divers. A second boat, the fifty-foot *Lutfi Gelil,* would be captained by Nazif Göymen, with Gunay Alpay as his crew. I was relieved to find that Nazif spoke some Greek, which I also knew from Athens; this would help while I began to learn Turkish.

Every foreign expedition is assigned a commissioner by the Antiquities Department, both to see that its work is legal and scientific, and to help with formalities and local logistics. Hakki Gültekin, director of the Izmir Museum, joined us as commissioner. We were doubly lucky. Not only did this mean that we were in business, that our permit was still valid, but kind-hearted Hakki Bey ("Mr. Hakki," the polite form of address in Turkey), was a rare combination of archaeologist and avid spear fisherman.

With Hakki Bey we discussed our plans for the summer. First we would sail south, to excavate the Bronze Age ship at Cape Gelidonya. Then we would return to Bodrum in order to excavate a Byzantine ship not far away.

The Lutfi Gelil *had been used in dragging for sponges long before being enlisted for archaeological research in 1960.*

We were six divers, plus Kemal's men, with a budget of $12,000, much of which had already gone for equipment, shipping, and transportation; and we planned to do it all in one summer.

"I'm going to take you spear fishing, George Bey," Peter said. It was *bayram,* a religious holiday, and there was little we could do to prepare for the trip south.

No sooner had we reached the castle, carrying fins and masks, than we were stopped by a policeman who threatened us with arrest if we entered the water. A copy of our excavation permit had not yet arrived at the police station, he said, and we could not begin our work until it had. We pleaded that we could not possibly be looking for wrecks just outside Bodrum harbor with snorkels, that we only wanted to go for a swim like any tourists. All was in vain.

Bodrum is small. Our Istanbul friends told us to be philosophical: "These men sit in this little town day after day, month after month, with almost nothing to do. Now you have arrived and they have something to do."

It had not helped that American divers had stolen objects from wrecks the year before and showed them on American television, leaving a justified cloud of suspicion that took us years to dissipate. It was especially hard on Peter, who was obsessed with the one thought of seeing that wrecks were excavated properly and their finds displayed in a museum in Bodrum; he had gone broke spending his own money on the idea. But rumors die hard: ten years later I was asked by a member of the American State Department if I knew "that fellow Throckmorton, the one who built a private museum for himself with all the stuff he took out of Turkey."

The policeman was overruled by a more sensible superior. Peter and I jumped off the mole blocking one side of Bodrum harbor. He grabbed the spear gun and I followed, gliding over the flickering, mottled landscape.

Suddenly Peter pointed at the rocks below, took a deep breath, and plunged straight for the bottom. So fast I could not grasp what was happening, a writhing dark mass twisted itself around the gun, straining upward, grasping for Peter's arm. My urge to rush to his aid and to back off at the same time left me treading water, wide-eyed and immobile, not realizing that Peter had captured an octopus. A black cloud of ink followed as he hauled it ashore and left it wet and quivering on the concrete mole.

After dropping the octopus off at a restaurant to be cooked for dinner, we walked around to the other side of the harbor. There the water was so shallow that we swam only four or five feet above the bottom. Again Peter pointed. Again he shot down and came up with a writhing, twisting object. Again I kept my distance. He held out a mottled yellow and brown moray eel several feet long. I waded ashore, no longer feeling very comfortable about putting my bare feet on the slippery rocks. The creature lay just a few feet away, speared through its head, as we warmed ourselves in the sun, had a cigarette, and dressed.

"What are you going to do with it now that it's dead?" I asked.

"He's dead, is he?" Peter smiled. "Do you have the jeep keys?"

He lifted the spear, the long speckled body hanging from it, and told me to dangle the keys above the eel's face. Powerful jaws snapped shut. The steel key came out dented with the marks of razor teeth.

If this was a dead moray, I didn't want to meet a live one. On that day my feeling for the sea changed, very slightly, forever.

A few nights later we made ready to sail. The Misses Taylor and Frost boarded the *Lutfi Gelil;* I was to travel on the flagship, *Mandalinçi,* and Peter, Dumas, and Hakki Bey were to drive the station wagon overland. Dumas, saying his good-byes, sat on the wooden roof of *Lutfi Gelil*'s engine room, unaware of the young mechanic below heating her diesel engine with a blowtorch—then the common method of starting Bodrum boats. The engine caught, a great explosion in its single cylinder sending a perfect smoke-ring out of the exhaust pipe and Dumas, in one nimble leap, far away on dry land. He mumbled something about how crazy we were to sail on a moonless night down the coast with captains who didn't even know how to read charts.

I sat by Kemal at the tiller for a long while, smoking and exchanging comments in my halting Turkish. The steady throb of *Lutfi Gelil*'s engine echoed our own over the water, as the lights of Bodrum blended with the stars and then faded behind us.

Finally I dropped into the cabin. It smelled of diesel oil, fumes, and something indefinable, which Peter once likened to old socks. An antique diving compressor took up most of the room. Smooth white ballast stones under my feet, I undressed and crawled onto the wooden shelf that served as a bunk, so cramped that I could raise my head only a few inches before bumping the deck beams. I knew it was the beginning of an adventure. I did not know that it was the beginning of a way of life. Rocked like a baby in a cradle, I fell asleep before I could think more about it.

A smooth day and night later we reached Finike, the town nearest Cape Gelidonya. For the first time the whole team met. We were anxious to get started. We had hoped to begin diving in early May and it was already June 10. But high winds and seas were to lock us in Finike for three long days—especially long since from there we could finally see it: the long finger of land stretching off into the distance, Cape Gelidonya. Out there, between two of the tiny islands all blurred together, lay the oldest shipwreck ever found.

CHAPTER II
Cape Gelidonya

CAPE GELIDONYA slopes gradually into the sea, a slanting field of grey stone spikes. The inhospitality of its shore is matched by that of the five islands that form a broken extension of the promontory. The edges of the islands are jagged knives of eroded rock where walking is all but impossible. Only eagles live in the towering crags above. We gave no thought to camping either on the cape, itself, or on the islands.

The search for fresh water—not only for drinking, but for washing corrosive salts out of whatever we might find on the wreck—led us nearly an hour's sail past Cape Gelidonya to a bay where Captain Kemal remembered two springs.

We sailed into an oven. The small bay faced south, and hundred-foot cliffs on all except its sea side closed out any breath of air and seemed to trap every degree of the sun's fierce rays. Along the back of the bay, gentle waves lapped a pebble beach only thirty feet wide. The springs were two unpromising damp patches of sand, separated by hundreds of tons of rock that had fallen across the beach, dividing it into two unequal lengths.

We spent the rest of the morning exploring even less inviting beaches, with Kemal doggedly holding to his first choice. Landslides might occur only when autumn rains loosened the rock, he reasoned, and the south wind, which would send waves racing across the beach, would come no sooner. I felt dubious about the whole situation as Nazif beached the *Lutfi Gelil* and we formed a human chain to unload the crates and trunks which, once unpacked, would be our only furniture. It was June 13.

Claude, an experienced mountaineer, clambered over the lower part of the cliff, driving in spikes from which we strung canvas flaps, parachutes, and tent fragments as awnings against the sun. Dumas, whom we were already beginning to call by his nickname Didi, set to work digging the moist patches of sand down to bedrock. We each took a turn and soon had two steady trickles which, dammed with stone and cement, formed knee-deep basins of clear, cool water.

Peter and Didi sailed next morning to locate the wreck and mark it with buoys while the rest of us stayed behind to complete the camp.

During our first night we had learned that an almost constant drizzle of tiny stones skipped down the sides of the cliff, and we hoped our frail barrier of canvas would offer at least some protection against their bigger brothers. We established separate "bedrooms" by dropping bare cot mattresses at random on the sand under the remnant of an old army mess tent. Kitchen, machine

We spent the first morning near Cape Gelidonya unloading crates of diving equipment onto a narrow beach that became our home for three months.

HERB GREER

shop, conservation laboratory, and breakfast room were simply areas of shade staggered along the beach. A small cave behind the dormitory tent was blocked with canvas to form a darkroom, with the sputtering generator for its enlarger placed as far away as our electric wire would allow.

The divers returned with discouraging news. They had found the wreck at once, but Peter felt that there was less material than he had remembered. He feared the cargo might have been robbed since his last visit.

The next day I made my first deep dive. Didi faced me, watching closely as we began to descend hand over hand, feet first, the weighted line from *Mandalinçi*. The water was so clear that the seabed ninety-five feet below was visible as soon as we put our heads under. On the bottom, Didi and Claude hovered around me like mother hens as I made my tour, memorable mainly in that I kept falling backward onto my tanks and then struggling, like a turtle, to right myself. It was my first look at an ancient wreck.

There was not much to see. The barrenness of the seabed, with only a few small fish to break the monotony, was accentuated by the monochrome green light. A flat rock platform, fifteen feet across and three feet higher than the surrounding sand bottom, joined the base of an underwater cliff that rose up to form the island by which we were anchored. A huge boulder, aptly described by Peter as being "big as a truck," had fallen nearby, leaving a narrow passageway only five feet wide between itself and the cliff base. Outside the boulder and the platform, and between them, was a light, sandy bottom which sloped off and disappeared into deeper water. Everything but the sand was covered with a dark sea growth.

Didi pointed out a stone mortar and a discus-shaped metal ingot lying loose, and fragments of fiber and broken metal tools in a small pocket of sand in the platform. The clearest evidence of there having been a wreck at all was left by what had already been removed: white impressions in the dark growth, like giant footprints, showed where four-handled copper ingots had been pried loose the previous summer.

It was not until four days later that we got a hint of the full significance of the site.

Didi took a geologist's hammer down on an exploratory dive and chipped away part of the platform. It was not solid rock. Its top was a thick mass of metal cargo, camouflaged by a heavy, rocklike sea concretion. He moved into the gully between the boulder and the cliff and found another thick deposit of metal, including whole ingots and bronze tools, again covered with a crust of concretion.

That night I excitedly wrote the news back to Dr. Young in Philadelphia: "He estimates it as at least a ton of material. So it looks like the Byzantine wreck must wait for another year, as we cannot get the things loose easily. Is this not the largest hoard of Bronze Age bronzes yet found?"

We could have begun ripping out objects and raising them to the surface immediately, for a hoard of this magnitude in itself would have been of scientific value. But archaeology is more than salvage.

As on land, the site had to be dissected carefully, so that the spacial relationships between objects could be observed and evaluated. Once excavated a site is destroyed forever. All that remains, besides a collection of artifacts, are the plans and records that allow the archaeologist to publish his evidence so that others can judge his interpretations and conclusions. Only then can the results become a new paragraph or page in history books.

Our immediate task then was to make an accurate plan of the site. Honor had brought sheets of frosted plastic paper, which she attached to a clipboard and drew on with an ordinary lead pencil under water. This was suitable for recording small assemblages of material, but for an overall plan of the site we needed something more. We took turns holding the end of a meter tape as she took measurements of the visible remains.

At the same time we attempted an "aerial survey." Didi marked the borders of the wreck and its more obvious features with white stones, which showed up well in photographs. Peter hovered over them, a plumb line attached to his camera so that he could stay a fixed distance above, while Claude swam beneath him, moving a calibrated surveyor's rod into each picture for scale. Herb worked far into the night in his tiny cavern, developing and printing the results of each day's "flight" with warm sea water.

The patchwork quilt we put together from the pictures showed little more than I had seen on my first dive, but it helped us to orient ourselves and plan each day's work. For years afterward I turned again and again to that first, crude photo-mosaic, which remained the only true picture of the site almost as it was first found.

Diving quickly became routine. Peter, Didi, and Claude posi-

Part of the Bronze Age ship had settled between the boulder and a cliff, just out of view on the right. Duthuit draws on frosted plastic paper.

HERB GREER

tioned an oil-drum buoy on the surface above one end of the wreck so *Mandalinçi* or the *Lutfi Gelil* could moor quickly each morning. I learned not to topple over on my back, and a week after my first dive I wrote to Dr. Young that the diving was going well. "It is rather tense work," I added, "and I think that people are less likely to be in a friendly mood after a dive. Our recompression chamber is still in customs and I, for one, do not enjoy the first hour after a long dive waiting to see if I shall come up with a case of bends." Each of us dived twice a day whenever possible, and we were totally isolated from medical facilities.

Hoes, axes, picks, adzes, and other tools began to litter the bottom of the fresh-water basin, along with ingots and ingot fragments. Miss Taylor (she was always "Miss Taylor" to us then) chipped and

Nearly thirty-two centuries ago a merchant ship had struck the jagged rocks and sunk to the seabed directly below the Lutfi Gelil's *mooring.*

chiseled the concretion away from the bronzes, and dunked fragments of pottery into various acid baths. The character of the cargo became clearer with each dive. I continued my reports back to Dr. Young:

June 27, 1960

The wreck seems to have been of a junk ship, carrying a load of old metal objects. Although we are getting many different kinds of copper ingots and spear points and agricultural tools, most of them seem to have been already broken when the ship was sailing. A great quantity of the cargo was just plain pieces of broken ingots. These pieces were either wrapped in baskets or, less likely, were lying on a woven mat over the deck.

Work was often tense without adequate equipment.
Claude Duthuit, Peter Throckmorton, Frederic
Dumas, and Honor Frost rest between dives.

HERB GREER

We have labeled the conspicuous objects, which must be lifted, and these are plotted on the plans. Then we go down with a draftsman and tie numbered plastic labels on the things I want lifted. These are then placed into a steel-wire basket and lifted with the hoist on the boat. So far most of the lifting has been of loose ingots and objects. To get into the heart of the ship will be a different matter. We have tried loosening objects under water and have made sets of chisels, crowbars, masons' hammers, and the like. But under water there is simply not enough time and it is easier to break something accidentally than on land. Therefore we have decided to try to raise one piece of concreted cargo all at once. To break it loose Dumas and Duthuit have been picking under the concretion, but it would take them months to loosen a very small section of just one area of the ship. Tomorrow they will try to use a car jack to break it loose.

Two days later we got our first taste of things to come:

June 29, 1960
If this letter reaches you in a bottle, fear for the worst. Our little beach is only about twenty feet wide and the south wind, which Kemal says never comes in the summer, came today. We had wet feet eating supper, and if the waves rise the slightest bit more, we will be floating out of here.

Today we got a jack under a large hunk of unintelligible concretion and cracked it loose. We then raised it with a cable and winch on the ship. After a bit of chiseling it turned out to be a stack of at least six, and maybe more, ingots of various shapes. Between two of the ingots a basket had been crushed, with rope and matting perfectly preserved.

Our food is now quite good. I will send a boat to Antalya every week if at all possible. I went the other day and found that they have every kind of fresh fruit and vegetable imaginable. Finike simply could not support us without a refrigerator. We lived on tomatoes and cucumbers for a week, with a little cheese, olives, and bread, and had yogurt once and meat once. The only other protein we had was the fish that we could spear during the evening. The whole crew was getting pretty weak, for diving really takes it out of you, and I think that is why I came down with some bug. As a matter of fact, I am going to send the whole crew into

Antalya this weekend for a day, for we have worked steadily for over two weeks without a single morning's break. I think that a day off every two weeks would be a good thing, although most of us want to keep working every day now that we have so little time left and there is the very real fear that someone else will come and tear up the rest of the ship if we do not finish the job.

Most of the team did go into Antalya for the weekend, but it was for the last time—our next day off was on September 13, the day we broke camp and left the site.

I stayed behind with Claude, to work on records, but I told Peter

Frederic Dumas uses a crowbar to pry one concreted mass of metal cargo from the seabed. The handle of an automobile jack, also used, protrudes in the foreground.

PETER THROCKMORTON & HERB GREER

to keep an eye out for Ann. She was to join me, but where? Peter conjured up a picture of her on a dusty road somewhere in Central Anatolia, asking every camel driver in a sweet southern voice: "Kin you all tell me the way to *Feeniky?*"

Peter spotted her in Antalya, which she had just reached by bus. That night she made her first acquaintance with a one-lung diesel engine as the throbbing deck of the *Lutfi Gelil* served as her pillow. I swam out to meet the boat next morning, wondering if she would recognize me with a full red beard, and wondering where we would live. Claude, the gallant Frenchman, insisted that Ann and I take his pup tent, the only one in camp, as our honeymoon bungalow.

The crates of fresh vegetables and fruit they brought back from Antalya were welcome relief, and we had visions of a healthy diet for the rest of the summer. But by now it was reaching 110° F. in the shade by ten in the morning, and we had no refrigerator. Nazif, who doubled as camp chef, immodestly fighting the heat in his immense underdrawers, cooked meat as soon as it arrived, salted it heavily, and then rinsed and recooked it each day. Even so, by the third day it was always rather special.

One or the other of our two boats was frequently *bozuk* with engine trouble, which meant we had to choose between diving and sending the only other boat to Finike for fresh supplies on any given day. We always preferred to continue working. On the worst day Claude asked what was for breakfast.

"Nothing," was my honest reply.

"C'mon, what's for breakfast?"

"Malaria tablets and tea."

We dived on nearly empty stomachs.

July 6, 1960

Compressor trouble is killing us. One still remains in customs, with Hakki Bey there now working to get it out. Our big compressor is still not working, but will fill the tanks enough for short dives. Peter's old compressor is at the mechanic's. Luckily two Germans and an American arrived the other day and asked to work with us for a week and they have a small compressor that is good for a few tanks a day, which is a help.

We continued to break loose great lumps of concreted cargo, sending them to the surface with cable and winch. Instead of chiseling

In order to raise heavier masses of concreted cargo, divers used one or more lifting balloons that were carried to the sea floor deflated, tied to the required object, and then filled with air from a diver's mouthpiece or spare tank. This small balloon can raise three hundred pounds.

out the encased objects immediately, as we had done with part of the first, we now took the lumps intact back to camp. There we fitted them together again, exactly as they had been on the seabed, heaving and straining and skinning our knuckles on the three-hundred-pound pieces of our back-breaking jigsaw puzzle.

The positions of the lumps on the seabed had been plotted on our plans, and once we had several joined together we began the slow process of knocking away the concretion to find what lay inside. Using sandbags to hold objects in position, we eventually had dozens of clean artifacts resting on the beach in exactly the same positions that they had held in the ancient merchantman three

Broken lumps of concreted cargo were fitted back together on land, by the author, Claude Duthuit, Wlady Illing, and Peter Throckmorton.

HERB GREER

millennia before. Drawn and photographed in place, they were finally separated and placed into the fresh-water pool to soak.

Sticking out from below a mass of concretion in the "gully" between boulder and cliff were pieces of wood that we assumed, at first, to be part of the ship. Then we noticed that they were sticks and twigs with the bark still well preserved. This brushwood posed a special problem. If we had tried to raise the concreted cargo resting on it with a cable, and had the boat above rolled even slightly, the heavy mass would have risen just an inch or two above the seabed and then come crashing down with destructive force. Dumas had a solution. He had brought two lifting balloons, each

When cleaned of concretion, ingots and tools retained on land the positions they had held for three millennia on the seabed.

PETER DORRELL

able to raise three hundred pounds. These he took down deflated, tied to the lump of cargo, and filled with air from his mouthpiece until the mass was neutrally buoyant. Then he eased the concretion away from the fragile wood and, with a final burst of air, sent it to the surface. We hooked it and pulled it aboard the *Lutfi Gelil.*

Many of the smaller items on board the ancient ship had filtered down into the thin layer of sand on the seabed before becoming

The two air lifts used at Cape Gelidonya: the taller of the two, placed in the gulley between boulder and cliff, emptied into the Lutfi Gelil.

ERIC J. RYAN

encased in concretion, and we searched for these by hand, sifting slowly with out fingers. Dumas was expert at it, and I learned from him how to form gentle currents with my hands, sweeping sand in any direction without disturbing the surrounding areas. Still, the work went too slowly.

In spite of the possible danger it presented to the wreck site, Peter and I decided that we must try the air lift, a kind of suction pipe, a month after we had begun the excavation. Our air lift was a fifty-foot tube of rigid metal sections with a flexible lower end of reinforced rubber. We buoyed the top of the tube fifty feet above the wreck with air-filled jerry cans, and weighted the lower end so that it floated upright. Air pumped down to its lower end through a small hose entered the pipe and burst into bubbles which, rushing up through the pipe, caused a great suction at its bottom.

Used gently, our underwater vacuum cleaner worked like a feather duster. In the first pocket of sand we cleared with it, near the boulder, we found a number of balance-pan weights, a bronze bracelet, a complete axe, and a whole chisel, all in perfect condition.

Wlady Illing, one of two German boys who had joined us earlier for a week, drove back from Germany to work with us the rest of the

We removed the thin covering of sand from the remains at Cape Gelidonya with an air lift, a kind of underwater vacuum cleaner.

HERB GREER

summer. He was an awesomely powerful diver who could swim down without equipment, holding his breath, and nonchalantly shake hands with us on the wreck a hundred feet deep. He told us that once he had passed out at that depth, struggling to pull a speared grouper from a cave, and somehow floated to the surface alive. His muscles added an extra lifting machine to our equipment; at the same time he was unusually delicate when working on the bottom.

A few days after we began air-lifting he spotted our prize object, a finely carved cylinder seal of the type used by Near Eastern merchants to sign clay documents or seal precious goods. Delicately carved on the dark, tiny stone, only an inch long and no larger than a pencil in diameter, were two turbaned Semites with long robes facing an unknown god wearing Egyptian dress and crown; birds and animals filled the background. I wondered if its owner was lost with the ship or, somehow, had returned safely to his home.

We needed still more divers. A fishing boat, its engine broken, was rowed into our bay in the middle of a black night, and two more waded ashore: Eric Ryan, a young art professor at Colgate University who had spent summers diving alone around Greece, and Yüksel Eğdemir, a member of the Türk Balikadamlar Kulubu.

Fresh faces picked us up. The old hands were wearing down. We couldn't decide which was worse, the heat or the flies. It became almost impossible to work on the plans during the day. Sweat poured off onto the paper, raising little blisters and smearing the ink. Flies crawled into our ears, over our lips, and bit our arms and hands as we drew. Our ankles were raw. We became maniacal killers, swatting flies by the hundreds and inventing all sorts of fly traps with sugar and water and tea glasses and paper cones. We couldn't dent the numbers, but it gave us the satisfaction of revenge. Terry Ball, a talented English artist whom Miss Taylor had sent for to draw objects, found just enough mosquito netting to make a cage for himself three feet high and long enough to stretch out his legs with a drawing board resting on them. For hours at a time he sat hunched over his work, trying to ignore the aching muscles in his back. Object photographer Peter Dorrell, who had accompanied him from England, found the emulsion peeling off all his films from heat. Our feet had built up thick soles of leather from weeks of going barefoot, but we still could not take more than a couple of steps on the baking pebbles. At night we plunged repeatedly into the sea and then flopped, still wet, onto our mattresses to try to catch a few hours' sleep.

Divers grew thin from constant work and lack of food. Claude lost thirty pounds, probably the average for all of us. Cuts and bruises never healed from constant immersion in sea water. Small scratches festered down to the bone and became just another attraction for flies.

Still, the divers were lucky. Almost every day we sailed out into the open, onto the sea, leaving Miss Taylor and Ann in the buzzing inferno to clean and catalogue our growing collection of bronzes; sometimes Honor took the outboard back from the site to join them, to try to get a little work done on the plans.

Ann Bass and the author use chemical preservatives to coat some rare fragments of wood from the Bronze Age shipwreck.

PETER THROCKMORTON

Some days the sea was rough. The bows of the *Lutfi Gelil* crashed through whitecaps as we commuted to work, sending sheets of water over us as we huddled under canvas in her open hold. Bobbing and rolling above the wreck, we looked forward to those few minutes each day when we slipped beneath the waves to work in the calm below. On one of the worst days I was especially glad to join Herb and Didi in that peaceful world.

Suddenly the quiet was broken by muffled shouts in the water. We looked up and saw Claude swimming rapidly toward us, gesturing urgently for us to surface. His Gallic hands explained his mission with complete clarity as we ascended: Nazif had cut off part of a finger in a loop of cable suddenly tightened by the heaving boat.

Peter and Miss Taylor (on a rare visit to the site) had already stopped the bleeding and applied bandages. Kemal laughed, said Nazif was stupid, and held up his own hand which lacked a joint. Peter and I tried to console Nazif with a cigarette and a shoulder to lean on. The *Lutfi Gelil* plodded slowly back toward the camp and our "hospital"—a trunk of medical supplies.

On the usually deserted horizon a fleet of sailboats was just visible. Kemal ran our Turkish flag to half-mast, a signal of distress. To my surprise, someone spotted it immediately. Looking like an ancient pirate fleet in the distance, the boats, Bodrum spongers on their way home, turned and sped toward us. The captains shouted back and forth over the rising wind as they brought their vessels dangerously close. The fastest threw a line and towed us quickly back to camp where we cleaned the wound and bandaged it again before sending Nazif to the doctor in Finike.

A week later Nazif was on the job again, minus his fingertip, but machines were more overworked and damaged than men. All of the compressors finally died and we were no longer able to fill tanks. I kept Peter and Kemal company as they tinkered and hammered and soldered by the flickering light of a gas lantern; I could offer nothing more than moral support, and that was not good enough. We needed spare parts. The excavation came to a halt.

We thought of *Mandalinçi*'s old diving compressor. It powered the air lift and supplied air to Kemal's helmeted sponge divers the few times they helped with heavy work on the wreck. But it wasn't a high-pressure compressor for filling tanks, and we had neither suitable hose nor fittings to adapt it to our equipment.

Peter sent to Antalya for an assortment of plumbing, and we

rigged two lengths of air-lift hose, comparable in strength and quality to garden hose, to the compressor on Mandalinçi. We attached a regulator and mouthpiece to the opposite end of each hose so that a pair of divers could now receive air pumped from the surface rather than from tanks on their backs. Gaskets were made from old shoes.

The flexible hose often kinked in the current, cutting off one's air supply on the bottom. Usually the kink came out if the diver rose

A hose from a shipboard compressor, rather than metal tanks, supplies Claude Duthuit's regulator with breathing air as he jumps overboard carrying metal detector and batteries. Excavators using this hookah, *or* narghile, *system of diving were not restricted by the limited amount of air in tanks.*

PETER THROCKMORTON

a few feet, but sometimes two of us had to ascend trading one mouthpiece back and forth. Luckily both hoses never kinked at the same time.

Dumas told us we were foolhardy, and at last refused to dive with our makeshift apparatus.

It *was* idiotic. The current runs between the islands at up to three knots and more according to official surveys of the region. Diving with aqualungs was difficult at best. Diving with the drag of a hundred feet of hose was insane. But we had no choice. We descended the shot line, our bodies flapping horizontally like flags in a wind, scarcely able to hold on. On the bottom we pulled ourselves from rock to rock over the site, never letting go. For forty minutes at a time one of us would brace his knees against one rock outcrop and his back against another so our hands would be free to hold Honor's hose while she measured and drew. Sometimes, more stupidly, we dived alone, and my closest call came when I began to black out from insufficient air while struggling to move the air lift against the current. I had only presence of mind to hold on tight, close my eyes, and relax until I could catch a few deep breaths.

July 30, 1960

Found three scarabs (two faience, one ivory) with hieroglyphic inscriptions, and a polished stone mace-head. Have about two hundred numbered objects now, including a bronze spade I hadn't mentioned. It looks now as if we are entering the "captain's cabin" with mace-head, scarabs, many more weights; I expect more.

We did find more. The "captain's cabin," as we called it, lay between the boulder and the cliff, near the spot where our air lift had uncovered complete tools rather than scrap. Along with more scarabs, unworked rock crystal, whetstones, and another mace-head, there appeared evidence of food—fish bones, olive pits, and a knucklebone from a sheep or goat—concreted under bronze cargo. Just above was the only lamp found on the wreck, a round and shallow saucer with pinched rim to hold a floating wick in place.

Life in the camp then remains a blurred series of impressions: Claude strolling down the beach, arms flailing the air like a bikinied Elmer Gantry, shouting "I got sex and religion, I got sex and religion;" Eric forming a one-man rescue party to bring Ann down from halfway up the cliff face where she had chased dinner, in the shape of two nimble-footed goats Nazif had bought from a visiting shepherd boy; Honor finding a fallen boulder on her mattress one night, just where she usually rested her head; the female rabbit we called John who lived on watermelon rinds; the landslide that sent us fleeing into the sea one midnight; all of us singing "Yellow Polka Dot Bikini" at the top of our lungs as we set sail in the morning.

The crew dwindled as Honor, Didi, Miss Taylor, Eric, and Yüksel had to return to their various jobs. The museum trustees had voted us an additional $6,000, and the American Philosophical Society had given $1,000, so we had money to continue, but by the end of August it was time for me to return to university classes. I asked Dr. Young for a reprieve:

September 4, 1960
By now you must have received my cable asking for a delay in my return. The reason . . . is that for about three solid weeks we have done nothing but cut through marble with sledgehammer and chisels, trying to free the one lump that seems to preserve part of the hull . . . We dive two at a time, twice a day—the first dive for forty minutes and the second for twenty-five.

A few days later, Nixon Griffis, a recent arrival, Peter, and I broke loose the stubborn "hull lump," and raised it to the surface. Luis Marden of the *National Geographic* luckily paid a two-day visit just then, bringing a metal-detector which enabled us to make a last,

Only in breaking loose the stubborn lump that held part of the ancient ship's hull were Kemal's helmeted sponge divers effective in the excavation.

thorough search for bronzes under sand and concretion.

Our dining table and benches, made from the air-lift crate, had long since washed away in the constantly rising water as the prevailing summer winds were replaced by the southerly *lodos* of fall. Now divers were wakened by water running around them under the tent. We moved the finds and equipment as high up on the rock falls as we could, and hoped the weather would not get worse for at least a few more days.

Gunay stood with trousers rolled above his knees, leaning into the surf to wash the dishes as he had all summer, but now wave after wave rose and pushed him back, soaking his body. He looked imploringly at Ann.

"Let us go from this place!" he cried, in the longest and most perfect English sentence he had spoken all summer.

The end came suddenly. I was feverish and could barely swallow from tonsillitis. Claude volunteered to give a penicillin shot. No sooner was I asleep than the entire camp was up.

"Rain is coming," Kemal said. It was still dark.

Before the sun rose we had completely dismantled our home of three months and packed every item of the camp onto the two boats. At dawn we sailed out of the little bay and took a last look at our lonely beach. Now it swarmed with people looking to see what we had been doing, looking to see if we had left anything of interest.

We were awakened by waves washing beneath our beds. Claude tries vainly to protect the camp as Yüksel Egdemir and Herb Greer watch helplessly.

PETER THROCKMORTON

With the exception of a single shepherd boy who had somehow scrambled down the cliff weeks before, these were the first outsiders we had seen on the beach all summer. Had they been watching us day and night?

We managed to reach Finike just before the first, violent storm of the fall.

We had permission from Ankara to start a little museum in the dining hall of the crusader castle, as Peter had hoped, and once back in Bodrum we set masons to work building concrete tanks to hold the ton of salvaged bronze and copper in fresh water during the winter. Other workmen built shelves and work tables, and laid a stone floor.

All this was anticlimactic. We were sore, tired, and thin. Worse, we had been away from outside human contact for too long.

Peter and I walked to the end of the dock and sat under the stars on the great breakwater that shelters Bodrum harbor. We talked about the Byzantine ship and how it should be excavated. By the end of the summer at Gelidonya, Peter was working around the clock mending machines, keeping notes for his book, and running the diving; he barely had time for photography, his profession. I said that next time we should have a professional mechanic and another professional photographer. I probably said it badly. It sounded to Peter as if I were criticizing his abilities. We both had the same aim: to see that the next job was as perfect as possible. But it all fell apart that night. We had a violent, nasty argument. After three months of confinement to a narrow strip of broiling beach we let our tempers pour out. Neither of us was right. We were arguing about nothing.

That was how it ended, the first scientific excavation of an ancient ship, the oldest ever found, even to this day. One by one we drifted away. Claude went as far as the Greek island of Cos with Ann and me and then returned to Bodrum where he and Wlady would continue cataloguing the finds.

CHAPTER III
East vs. West

~~~~~~~~~~~~~~~~~~~~~~~~~~~~
~~~~~~~~~~~~~~~~~~~~~~~~~~~~
~~~~~~~~~~~~~~~~~~~~~~~~~~~~

THE excavation was over, but work on the wreck had scarcely begun. Field work takes only a small percentage of an archaeologist's time, but, like the tip of an iceberg, it is the part that attracts notice. Laymen seldom realize that the more rewarding part is invisible, hidden away in library stacks and museum basements. If it is exciting to find an ancient object, how much more so to discover when it was made and where, who used it and how, and what new knowledge of our past it contains. The infrequent finds of glittering jewelry and virgin tombs that make headlines lead to misunderstanding of how an archaeologist spends most of his time.

Now, from a ton of corroded metal, shattered pottery, and fragmentary wood we hoped to learn the story of a ship: How was it built? When did it sink? What was its purpose? Its route? Its nationality?

Could we somehow revive from its lifeless remains an unrecorded moment from three millennia before?

As soon as Ann and I returned to Philadelphia, I gave myself completely to the attempt. The clues from the sea remained in

Bodrum. I worked with surrogates, in the form of drawings, photographs, measurements, and written descriptions.

Of the ship itself we could say little. Once she had been alive, cloth lungs filled to bursting with air, her sinews of twisted fiber alternately tensing and relaxing as she complained aloud under the strain. But the scattering of sand on which she ultimately fell still, offered scant covering for a burial. Exposed and vulnerable, her body was consumed by the worms of the sea, leaving only patches of wooden skin protected under the weight of copper and bronze ingots.

The extent of this metallic offal suggests that she had been about thirty-five feet in length, the size of *Mandalinçi* and the Aegean boats whose sails less than a century ago dotted the Mediterranean on annual pilgrimages to the sponge fields of North Africa.

Her delicate planks were pinned together with wooden pegs and covered by a protective layer of twigs in her bilge, in the manner described by Homer (but usually mistranslated from his Greek). The double-bladed axe and adzes of bronze she carried matched the tools Odysseus used to build his craft.

That she sailed during the age of Homer's heroes, there is no doubt. The jugs and jars on board were of a style considered fashionable around 1200 B.C., give or take fifty years, and Troy was sacked at some time, still debated, between the early thirteenth and early twelfth centuries B.C.

The dating of the pottery reached me from London, where Joan Taylor worked with duplicate sets of photographs and drawings. At the same time, an independent dating was being made in Philadelphia at the University Museum's Carbon-14 Laboratory. In its first room, a chamber of steaming liquid-oxygen vats and dripping glass retorts, a sampling of brushwood dunnage from the ship's bilge was cleansed in acids. Then, somewhere in the maze of pipes and tubing, which spread over the room like a glassblower's folly, it was incinerated. Gases trapped from this graceless cremation were placed in the grey-walled cell of lead bricks, which dominated the second room. A Geiger counter, in ceaseless intermittent clicks, ticked off the degree of radioactivity inside. The amount allowed physicist Beth Ralph to calculate the length of time since the twigs had died. While alive, like all living things, they had absorbed minute amounts of the radioactive carbon constantly produced in the air by the bombardment of cosmic rays from outer space. Once cut for use on the ship, they had ceased to breathe. Beth measured how far back the radiocarbon had begun to decay. Her results were identical to Joan Taylor's: 1200 B.C. plus or minus fifty years.

The metal cargo did not immediately suggest to me that a tinker, or itinerant smith, had sailed on our ship's last voyage. It was a conclusion reached in stages.

I began a study of the copper ingots, those strange, four-handled slabs shaped like rigid first-aid stretchers, their dull green patinas only a pin scratch away from the shiny metal beneath. I learned that similar ingots of the Bronze Age had been found from Mesopotamia to Sardinia, often pulled from the sea in the earlier decades of our century. They were called "ox-hide" ingots by students of ancient coinage, for with four "legs" and one rough "hairy" side they resembled dried cowhides with head and tails removed; they were thought to have been cast to the same shape and weight, each equaling the price of an ox or cow in the days before the invention of money.

A German scholar, Hans-Günter Buchholz, had made a careful study of such ingots. He had learned that they could be dated roughly by their shapes and the lengths of their handles, and had offered evidence that they were probably not cast intentionally to look like dried skins. I found additional evidence to support his theories.

Five minutes at the Kramer Ingot Company in Philadelphia showed me that, surprisingly, none of the scholars who had written about the ingots had ever watched molten metal being poured. The "hairy" side was the naturally bubbly upper surface of copper cooling in open air, not a lower surface formed in a purposely uneven mold; modern founders take care to prevent this rough surface by floating powdered charcoal on the liquid metal. Since the random weights of our ingots varying between thirty-five and fifty-seven pounds were based on no standard at all—another surprise—it was impossible that they had served as currency. There now seemed no reason to believe that the ingots were anything other than simple slabs of copper, their "legs" serving as handles for ease of porterage, to be melted down and mixed with tin to form bronze.

About the same time, laboratory analysis showed that a white, toothpastelike substance spread among the ingots on the seabed was the residue of tin ingots, the earliest ever found.

We now had proof that our ship carried the ingredients for making new bronze. Old bronze, in round bun-shaped cakes and broken tools, was simply to be recast. Still, there was nothing so far to indicate that any of this was for more than barter.

The smoothly polished stone mace-heads, which we surmised were symbols of authority for the officer of the ship, I next learned were quite similar to the hammers used today in primitive societies to forge bronze. A large, hard stone, flat on top, could have served as an anvil; on the other hand, it weighed exactly 73,900 grams (or 163 pounds), or about two talents—a talent being a weight used for metals in antiquity—and might have been used instead in the weighing of heavy cargo.

A double-bladed bronze axe was found with broken tools, probably carried as scrap. This adze, one of a number found, may have been for shipboard use.

PETER DORRELL

PETER DORRELL

Scrap metal was carried in wicker baskets. The bottom of one basket, crushed between two copper ingots, was protected from damage by shipworms.

The most common tools in the cargo of scrap metal on the Bronze Age ship were agricultural: hoes and plowshares.

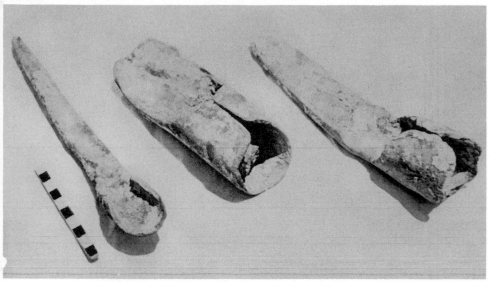

A perplexing block of bronze had caused unresolved speculation in the camp at Gelidonya. About four inches long, with one square end flat and the other concave, it was pierced by three tapered holes of differing size, and grooved on opposite sides with graded channels. Some had guessed that it was broken from something larger, others that it was complete. Now I stumbled on a woodcut of something vaguely similar in an 1881 publication titled, accurately but unimaginatively, *The Ancient Bronze Implements, Weapons, and Ornaments of Great Britain and Ireland.* It did not offer positive identification, but prompted me to post a photograph of our puzzle immediately to Paul Shaw in Annapolis, Maryland. Paul, an expert metal worker, is descended from English blacksmiths. By return mail he identified the block as a swage, a small, anvil-like tool used for bending and shaping metal in its various grooves and holes.

The swage from Cape Gelidonya was not unlike those used today for shaping metal implements.

Finally there were the whetstones and stone polishers from the "captain's cabin," far too numerous to be explained easily by any other logic than that dozens of new bronze blades were to be sharpened before the voyage was over.

None of this proved the presence of a seaborne tinker. But I could almost feel his presence.

The ship, floating foundry or not, was last laden on Cyprus. Of that I felt quite certain. Our broken, abandoned tools, some branded with signs from the still undeciphered script of Bronze Age Cyprus, are identical twins of implements unearthed on the island, where the molds of stone and metal in which they were created were also found. Ore for the copper ingots almost surely had been mined from the rich veins still exploited there.

But what of the home port? Cargo does not denote the nationality of a ship. Was ours Cypriot, Egyptian, Syrian, Cretan, or Greek?

I still assumed, as did we all, that our ship was Mycenaean—that is, from Greece in the Late Bronze Age, when Agamemnon ruled from the towering stronghold at Mycenae. It was fairly well accepted among historians that Mycenaean shipping dominated the Eastern Mediterranean during this period, from 1600 B.C. until the turbulent years around 1200 B.C., and that Semitic maritime commerce did not begin seriously until several centuries later when seafaring Phoenicians, descendants of the Canaanites of Syria, began their westward expansion. Homer's mention of Phoenician sailors in the Bronze Age, at the time of the Trojan War, was considered an anachronism of this later period in which he wrote, centuries after the events he described.

The cylinder seal and Syro-Palestinian scarabs lost at Cape Gelidonya, if this were true, were simply trinkets picked up by Greek sailors at some Near Eastern port.

Every Near Eastern merchant carried a seal for signing documents.

Scarabs carried by the Cape Gelidonya ship were made on the Syro-Palestinian coast in imitation of Egyptian scarabs.

It was, perhaps, when I completed a study of the balance-pan weights that this assumption began to bother me. I had divided the weights of each stone by consecutive numbers from one to sixty. As a result, several precise figures began to appear increasingly on the grids and tables I prepared: about a dozen weights seemed to be exact multiples of 9.32 grams, the weight of an Egyptian *qedet,* a common standard in Syria, Cyprus, Palestine, the Hittite Empire, Troy, and possibly Crete and Greece. Others were based on the so-called Phoenician standard of 7.32 grams, used in Egypt, Syria, Palestine, and Crete. Syrian *nesefs* of 10.30 grams, and Hebrew *shekels* of 11.50 grams also came to light in the grids.

If maritime trade was entirely in Aegean hands at this time, why did merchants as far west as Crete use weight systems whose origins were almost wholly Near Eastern?

I took another look at the cargo of four-handled ingots. From the day I met Peter, I had known that similar ingots were painted on the wall of at least one Egyptian tomb, carried effortlessly on the shoulders of a static procession of rigid porters. Hieroglyphs identify the scene as tribute brought to the pharaoh by the chiefs of Keftiu.

The ingot-bearers from Keftiu are bare but for richly patterned kilts and boots. Their skins are dark red. Jet black hair tumbles in long strands nearly to their waists. They are clean shaven.

They remind us of Minoans, the thalassic race who once graced Crete. We know Minoans from frescoes and ivory carvings in their sprawling island palaces where, with the sea like a protective moat, they were free to prosper and develop creativity to its fullest. Minos, their king, is credited with forming the first navy, which carried commerce and colonists to distant shores, and swept the Mediterranean of pirates. Then, in the second half of the fifteenth century B.C., their brilliant civilization was nearly extinguished by unknown forces. Does the legend of Theseus sailing from Greece to

Balance-pan weights of haematite, a reddish brown stone, were polished to a smooth accuracy in various Near Eastern weight standards.

slay the Cretan Minotaur echo a sudden destruction of Minoan power by Mycenaean warriors? Was the island already weakened by giant tidal waves sent coursing over its coasts by the epochal eruption on neighboring Thera—perhaps giving rise to the story of Atlantis?

Because the Egyptian tomb-painting of ingots from Keftiu is the most commonly reproduced picture of ingots from ancient art, and because Keftiu is believed to have been the Egyptian name for Crete, most archaeologists guessed that ingots were Cretan, or at least Aegean, objects of trade. Ignored by them was a lower row of ingot-bearers in the same painting: brown-bearded Syrians in long, white robes.

Even if ingots were bartered mainly by Cretan merchants during the heyday of Minoan civilization—and the evidence seemed ambiguous—did this important trade necessarily pass into Mycenaean hands afterward?

I wondered if more evidence might exist. Ann and I began a search for ingots in Egyptian tomb paintings and sculptured reliefs. There was no bibliography to guide us, and even the indices at the backs of books were of little help; often ingots were not mentioned at all, or they had been wrongly identified as sacks. There was only one course to follow: to try to examine every illustration in every book on Egypt in the University Museum.

Ann often stayed with me through the night in the Egyptian seminar room. We grew to know the night watchmen better than anyone else in the museum, sharing coffee at midnight and looking forward to the apples that Ernie, the last guard to come on duty, frequently brought us in the early morning hours.

After we had finished in the seminar room, we scanned the journals of the main museum library—anything that might have a reproduction of an Egyptian painting. I would start at one end of a shelf and Ann at the other, working our way toward the center. Some of the more esoteric titles I'd never heard of before.

By the time we had finished we had spotted sixteen paintings and reliefs showing ingots of the kind found at Cape Gelidonya. Only two showed ingots borne by men from Keftiu at all, and in both cases ingots were shown in the same scenes borne by men from North Syria; in one of these the copper was identified, in hieroglyphs, as being from the land of Retnu (North Syria). In both examples mentioning Keftiu, however, the paintings were made more than two centuries *before* the Gelidonya disaster, the period when Crete was still a major economic force in the eastern Mediterranean. In every other case where the origin of the ingots was given, in Egyptian writing, the source proved to be North Syria. One painting, in the tomb of a nobleman at Thebes, even depicted the Syrian ship that brought the copper to Egypt. There could be no doubt at all that Egyptians considered the ingots as primarily Syrian, and most probably solely Syrian by the time that the ship sank at Cape Gelidonya.

I looked again at the personal belongings carried on the ship. The lamp, stone mortars, and stone hammers were as Near Eastern in

A man from Retnu (Syria) bringing an ox-hide ingot as tribute to the king, in an Egyptian tomb painting of the fourteenth century B.C.

SUSAN WOMER,
AFTER DAVIES,
COURTESY METROPOLITAN
MUSEUM OF ART

The pinched rim of the ship's terracotta lamp held a wick that floated on oil in the bowl. The lamp is of typical Syro-Palestinian shape.

C.F. BASS

character as the seal and scarabs, but they were surely not merely souvenirs of a port call. They were meant for daily shipboard use. Why then was our seal not simply the personal signature of the ship's merchant? All Near Eastern merchants carried one. Even the pottery, although sometimes taking Aegean shapes, seemed mostly to have been manufactured on Cyprus or in the Near East. Among a ton of material, there was not one object which pointed to a Mycenaean home port.

Puzzling at first, all this made sense if the Gelidonya ship was Syrian or Canaanite. But was this of historical importance? One ship does not necessarily represent a seafaring nation. Perhaps our ship showed a solitary flag against a sea of competition.

A closer examination of the supposed Aegean maritime monopoly was needed. True, it existed in Greek tradition, but Near Eastern cuneiform tablets mention vast Near Eastern fleets in the same period; and foreign fleets depicted in Egyptian paintings were Syrian, never Aegean.

It was the quantity of Mycenaean pottery, found along the coasts and navigable rivers of Cyprus, Egypt, and Syria, which had fostered the prevailing view that Bronze Age commerce was almost entirely in the hands of Mycenaean traders; similar amounts of Near Eastern pottery were not found in Greece and the Aegean islands.

Pottery and its contents were not given out free, however. There was something traded in return. Something unrecognizable to archaeologists. Something perishable that did not come in pottery containers. Textiles? Timber? Grain?

What more valuable raw material was there than metal? Its origin would scarcely be recognized if found in a Mycenaean city, for most was cast into typically Mycenaean forms soon after arrival in Greece. Most of the few ingots and ingot fragments found in Greece, in fact, were in blacksmiths' hoards, lost or abandoned before being fashioned into finished products. Who traded these raw materials: Mycenaeans or Semites?

The question led to the reevaluation of another view which prevailed among many archaeologists. This held that Cypriot bronzework was largely Mycenaean in inspiration, a result of Mycenaean overseas expansion. I learned to my surprise, after a study of all Cypriot bronze types, that the earliest examples of implements that became common on Cyprus were found on the Syro-Palestinian coast, suggesting Near Eastern rather than Greek origins.

When our final report on the Cape Gelidonya ship was published by the American Philosophical Society seven years after the completion of the excavation, I concluded not only that the ship was Syrian, but that Semitic maritime activity was significant in the Bronze Age Mediterranean.

The debt of Classical Greece to the Near East for its intellectual and artistic gifts is universally accepted. From the exchange of goods and ideas between Greek and Phoenician merchants in the eighth and seventh centuries B.C., Greece received the alphabet, the concept of monumental stone sculpture, enriched pottery decoration, architectural ornamentation, and advanced techniques of jewelry, carving, and metalwork. It was a time when Phoenician craftsmen were especially welcomed in Greece for their skill as bronzesmiths.

I was suggesting that early Phoenician bronze merchants were making contact with Greece centuries earlier than previously recognized.

The conclusions were startling and controversial. Few traditionalists accept them. A photograph and drawing of every object from the wreck appears in the publication, with plans showing where they had been found on the site, and maps pinpointing where similar objects had been excavated on land. Each reader may decide for himself.

CHAPTER IV
Return to Bodrum

IN THE winter of 1960 I was still a student, with a full load of courses as well as research on Cape Gelidonya to occupy me, but I could not forget the Byzantine shipwreck near Bodrum. Peter had told me about it and shown me photographs, and I had dived on it twice with Mustafa Kapkin, Peter's partner in earlier exploration, at the end of the Gelidonya excavation.

It lay just off Yassi Ada, a speck of rock between the Turkish mainland and the Greek island of Kalymnos. One of perhaps a dozen ships that had ripped its bottom out on an underwater extension of the island, the Byzantine ship rested slightly deeper than the Bronze Age wreck, on a slope 100 to 125 feet down. Peter had found traces of wood just below the sand, and felt there was a good chance that a large part of the hull might be preserved. Just thirty or forty feet away, in slightly deeper water, was the cargo of a ship estimated to be a century or two older by the shapes of its wine jars.

When I had decided to go to Gelidonya it was because it was a Bronze Age site. I was specializing in Neolithic and Bronze Age archaeology and had no plans to continue underwater excavation simply for the sake of diving—not unless another pre-Classical wreck were found. But before we all left Bodrum a few months earlier, in the fall, Claude and Wlady had called me to their room.

"You've got to continue, George. We've started something good. You're the only archaeologist with the experience to do another wreck now. Don't let it all go to waste."

I knew almost nothing about Late Roman and Byzantine archaeology, and I would never have chosen to dig a Byzantine site on land. Why should I excavate a Byzantine ship?

It was not the Byzantine ship alone that made me decide to continue. Wlady and Claude were right. We did have to go on. Underwater archaeology held incredible promise, and there were so many mistaken ideas about it.

Ships have crossed the Aegean for at least nine thousand years. Even before Stone Age man in Greece conceived living in mudbrick villages, before he learned to fire pottery, before he knew of planting crops or herding animals, he regularly brought obsidian, a natural volcanic glass, back to the mainland from the island of Melos. We do not know what kinds of craft he used to fetch this raw material for blades and scrapers—rafts, boats, dugouts, skin floats? —but surely some of them sank.

How many craft have gone to the bottom since that first sailor set forth? Only ten disasters a year would total ninety thousand wrecks, but far more than ten a year occurred. More than six hundred Persian ships perished in but one year, 480 B.C., from two storms. How many more ships were lost that year in the Mediterranean— fishing boats, ferries, merchantmen, and warships?

Some were broken and scattered against rocky shores, but others became nautical time capsules. Virtually everything man has ever made, from intricate pieces of jewelry to huge marble blocks for temples and churches, has been carried at one time or another by water craft. On the bottom these cargoes, and the ships themselves if quickly shielded from worms by protective sand or mud, lay safely hidden from their worst enemy—man. On land he burned marble statues and temple columns for lime, melted down bronze and gold for new uses, and gathered ships' timbers for firewood.

A hint of the great archaeological wealth on the seabed came to light in the eighteenth century when a fisherman netted the bronze statue of a standing male youth, called *Apollo,* off the coast of Italy near Piombino. It was to become the finest piece of sculpture in the Louvre's Hall of Bronzes.

Other masterpieces followed. When I was a student in Greece, the only large Greek bronze statue that had *not* come from the sea was the *Charioteer* in the Delphi Museum. The *Marathon Boy,* the *Antikythera Youth,* and the great *Zeus* from Artemision, all on display in the National Museum in Athens, represented the cargoes of three different ships which had carried rare works of art to the bottom of the Aegean. Another wreck, near Mahdia in Tunisia, has filled several museum galleries with marble and bronze statuary. These were all chance finds of sponge divers and fishermen during the first three decades of the twentieth century. The discoverer lacked the means to attempt scientific excavation. Yet when an archaeologist became involved in their salvage operations he was a passive observer on the surface, accepting in gratitude the finds handed up to him.

With the invention of the aqualung in the 1940s, by Jacques-Yves Cousteau and Emile Gagnan in France, divers gained the necessary mobility for doing delicate work on fragile ships' hulls. Then a number of attempts were made along the coasts of France and Italy to excavate Roman ships. None was carried to completion. None resulted in a plan of the ship's remains, which would allow an accurate reconstruction. In no case did an archaeologist direct the excavation on the seabed.

Now instead of clumsy helmeted sponge divers, tethered to the surface, aqualunged divers, professional and amateur, held the monopoly on underwater research. But the work remained salvage, often no better than that done by the earlier spongers. This is not to deny the serious intent of some of the pioneers, and the advances they made in digging methods.

A great deal of nonsense was being written about the new field. Wanting to stake their claim on underwater archaeology, some divers made exaggerated statements about the difficulties of underwater work. Where was the archaeologist who could deny them? Before I went to Gelidonya, some of the veterans of past campaigns warned me not to expect to do a truly scientific excavation:

"There is no time under water. Time is money, and you must work fast to get the results as quickly as possible."

Even after we had finished at Cape Gelidonya, the first site to be excavated completely on the seabed, I read statements by some of the pioneers emphasizing that only professional divers could work properly under water, that it required many years of diving experience to understand ancient wrecks, that no archaeologist could possibly learn in just a few years to dive well enough to excavate under water; some even said that only men who had been reared in the Mediterranean were qualified for the job—immediately excluding all divers from England, Germany, Scandinavia, and the Americas!

Professionals may tend to stress the difficulty of their field, whatever it is, perhaps to justify their own possible mistakes, perhaps to frighten away competition. In underwater archaeology, if those whose skills were limited to diving were to admit that architects and photographers and archaeologists could learn to excavate wrecks together, what role would they have left for themselves?

The divers had now had their day, and scientific results were limited. They were the pioneers who made our work at Gelidonya possible, as I was the first to admit. I did not criticize their past mistakes. I only criticized the attitude that tried to prevent the archaeologists from having a try.

I began to lie awake at night, thinking of ways to excavate the Byzantine ship, to make it a model on which future excavations might be based. The greater depth of the wreck meant that we would have less time on each dive than at Cape Gelidonya, so there would have to be more divers. They would not be simply divers. They would be exactly the same sort of people who are found on any land excavation. I needed to find draftsmen, photographers, an architect, archaeologists, and a mechanic and doctor for our special needs. If they didn't know how to dive we would teach them.

A professor of classics at Swarthmore College mentioned a young undergraduate who wondered if she might work on our underwater project. At that time I couldn't be particular about experience or age.

Susan Womer arrived at my office a few days later. She wore knee socks and plaid skirt, and had blonde curly hair. She read in great seriousness a prepared list of questions. She said she would like to draw for us. She didn't know how to dive, but was willing to learn.

I had never "hired" anyone before. I told her to choose a Greek vase from the storage shelves in the corridor outside, and draw it. The results were superb; accurate and attractive. Susan began diving lessons with the Depth Chargers.

I went with Ann to a film Stanton Waterman had made of the 1959 search expedition, which Peter had guided. Afterward I waited at the front of the auditorium to meet him. Next to me stood a lean, slightly round-shouldered young man with horn-rimmed glasses. He wore a wide belt with ornate buckle that I later learned was from his days as a wrangler out West. He introduced himself: "Laurence T. Joline, *J-o-l-i-n-e.*"

He spoke clearly and deliberately, as he does everything. When he learned that I was continuing the work shown in the film he asked if he could come and talk to me about it. I was preoccupied with meeting Stan Waterman, but said he should drop around. Over coffee in the museum the next day, he volunteered that he might be able to help us. He was a good diver and could draw. I said we didn't really need divers, and we already had an artist. On his next visit he showed me biological drawings from his college days. He was polite but persistent. Finally I told him he could come with us if he, like Susan, could pay his own fare to Turkey and back.

A graduate student of linguistics at the University of Pennsylvania asked about our work. He couldn't come that year, but when he heard we wanted a doctor on our staff he told me that I might try his brother, Charles Fries, a professor of surgery in New York. Charles, or Chuck, agreed over the telephone to join us. We first met when he drove me to the Navy Diving School in New London, Connecticut, to talk with Commander George Bond about some of the medical problems we might face. While there we met Commander Robert Workman, and another visitor to the school, Hannes Keller. They were men calculating the tolerance of the human body to the stresses of submarine pressures, their names well known to anyone in the diving world. I felt out of place forming my little group of novices.

I worried a bit about Chuck. His waistcoat, neatly trimmed hair, and steel-rimmed glasses gave him an air of impeccability. I wondered how he would fit into our rugged and often dirty work.

A fellow student told me that there was another graduate student in our department of Classical Archaeology who was a fantastic diver, "dying to go" on our next expedition. I asked to meet him and was surprised to learn that he knew almost nothing about our work and had given no thought to joining us. His diving, in fact, was limited to a little snorkeling in the Pacific while he was in the army. But our conversation introduced me to Frederick van Doorninck, who signed on the team shortly afterward. He was reputed to have the best knowledge of ancient Greek of any student who had passed through the department.

David Owen, still in his teens, an undergraduate at Boston University, met me at a meeting of the Archaeological Institute of America. He thought that marine archaeology offered limitless possibilities, and had taken a diving course to prepare himself for it. Short, dark, bespectacled, with a moustache that has appeared and disappeared regularly since I have known him, he straddled a stool next to me in the hotel drugstore and quietly talked his way onto the expedition. He had no money, but borrowed his fare to Bodrum.

Claude had lined up Jean Naz as mechanic. Short and wiry, sprouting a scraggly Fu Manchu beard and moustache, Jean could repair equipment without tools or spare parts. Born in Indochina on his parents' plantation, he still bore scars from time spent as a POW during World War II. His parents had lost everything, but started from scratch to rebuild their fortune after peace came. When they were finally back on their feet, the Vietminh arrived; the family fled through a back window and watched their house razed. Both parents gave up and died soon after. Jean seemed to see only futility in material possessions and roamed between Paris and India, making documentary films and working at whatever pleased him. I doubt that he owned more than could go into a suitcase then.

Bill Wiener I knew only through correspondence. He had just graduated from the Cornell Department of Architecture and would be in charge of making our plans. He had dived a couple of times with a friend.

Claude Duthuit, Wlady Illing, Eric Ryan, and Herb Greer were to return with me as seasoned veterans from the Cape Gelidonya campaign. There wasn't a real professional among us. We were a group of students and amateur divers, thrown together almost by chance, hoping to prove what we could do.

Peter and I had long since patched up our Bodrum quarrel and were collaborating on the publication of the results we had obtained at Cape Gelidonya. We still hoped to work together at Yassi Ada, but this didn't work out and he went on to survey and excavate wrecks in Greece, where he had made his home, and in Italy.

We now had people. We needed equipment. And money. Dr. Froelich Rainey, director of the University Museum, said that the museum would again give financial support to an underwater excavation. Nixon Griffis and the American Philosophical Society agreed to continue their aid, and were joined by the Catherwood Foundation near Philadelphia. I approached the National Geographic Society, whose Research and Exploration Committee voted to give us a grant. The Bauer Compressor Company in Munich presented us with a new compressor for filling tanks. And the Main Line Diving Club of Philadelphia, in a most moving gesture, collected enough funds from its members to help fellow member Larry Joline get to Turkey and back.

Wlady returned to Bodrum in May, several weeks before the rest of us, and located a heavy wooden barge, about fifty feet long and twenty feet wide, which would serve as a stable diving platform. He also found two abandoned houses, which we would rent for living quarters—at ten dollars and fifteen dollars a month—and, soon joined by Herb and Larry, began to shovel out years of accumulated debris.

By the time I arrived, after a quick trip to Ankara to pick up the excavation permit, Ann, Susan, Fred, and Chuck were already settled in. Susan and Herb seemed to be competing for the championship in collecting bug bites from the derelict dwellings, their faces almost unrecognizable under masses of walnut-sized lumps. Not to be outdone, Herb had fallen from a ladder and cut off the end of a finger. Chuck had just arrived and was rushed from the bus, bags still unpacked, to the accident. The town generator had closed down for the night. Ann held a flashlight while Chuck searched for needle and thread in his medical kit and sewed up the damage.

For another month we toiled, hauling crates of equipment from Izmir, scraping and painting rusted metal tools from Cape Gelidonya, arranging the barge, and teaching newcomers to dive. These included Enver Bostanci, a noted prehistorian from Ankara University, who was to serve as commissioner; he would be assisted by Yüksel Eğdemir, now working for the Antiquities Department after his experience on our staff at Cape Gelidonya.

Kemal had sent *Mandalinçi* out sponging with his mate in charge, and had acquired *Sanane,* a fast, sloop-rigged motor-sailor. Eric, Yüksel, and I sailed with him to the wreck and placed a makeshift buoy so we could anchor the barge directly above.

Finally, the second week of July, all was ready. The barge looked like a floating gypsy camp, a mass of cots and crates and canvas flaps, piled high with compressors, tanks, generators, hoses, and pipes. In the dead of the first calm night we had had in many days, we scrambled aboard as *Sanane* and a Bodrum sponge boat began the slow sixteen-mile tow to Yassi Ada.

The island deserved its Turkish name: Flat Island. A mixture of grey and reddish-brown rock, it looked like a giant pancake risen slightly in the center. Only a few patches of green scrub brush, especially on its highest point, broke the bleakness of the terrain.

None of us slept. We were too excited. Next day would begin the test of what we could do.

CHAPTER V
Yassi Ada

"DROP the anchor!" Kemal shouted.

Links of rusty chain rattled across the deck, followed by the rasp of cable sawing wood. One hundred feet. Two hundred feet. The end whipped over the side of the barge and disappeared in the blue water.

Turkish, German, and English curses followed.

No one had fastened the end of the cable to the barge!

The massive, tar-blackened hull drifted slowly out toward the open sea. Kemal gave chase in *Sanane* and towed it back under the lee of Yassi Ada. We were all dead, coated with that dirty, unshaven feeling that only a razor and toothbrush could cure. We had spent the day jockeying the barge into position directly over the Byzantine shipwreck one hundred and twenty feet below. Now we would have to wait for morning to try again. At least we could sleep.

Shortly after dawn, Wlady and Eric strapped on tanks and went over the side. About fifty feet deep on the slope of the reef they found the cable, attached a light line and brought its free end back to the surface. We heaved on the line until we could grasp the end of the cable and wrap it around our winch.

"Vira!" Turn. *"Cek!"* Pull. We took turns at the heavy handles of the winch. Hundreds of pounds of cable and chain piled on the

splintered deck before we could reach down and throw a line around the anchor itself. We were ready to start again.

"Drop the anchor!" Kemal shouted.

Again the rapid *thnk, thnk, thnk* of chain, and the rasping of cable.

"Tamam. We're anchored."

The most scientific underwater excavation ever had finally begun.

We readied another cable that would run to Yassi Ada, about a hundred yards away. The barge moved astern with the light northwest breeze, toward a black rubber life-vest that marked the spot where it was to stop. We reached our flimsy buoy—and drifted on by. We still weren't anchored! Wlady put the tank on again.

This time he found the cable hanging below us like a great ball of tangled yarn, completely wrapped around the anchor. It had been let out so quickly it had formed this massive knot before the barge could take up any of the slack and pull the anchor fluke into the seabed.

"Vira! Vira! Vira!"

Loose strands of wire cut into our blistered hands. The dirty engine oil in which the cable had been pickled all winter spattered our clothes and was soon smeared from our hands to our faces. Larry used a shred of burlap as an enormous mitten and coiled the cable as best he could, taking up most of the strain and most of the oil and grease against his khaki trousers. The winch seemed harder and harder to turn. At last the anchor broke the surface.

"Drop the anchor!" Kemal shouted.

This time all our practice paid off. Everything went like clockwork. We ran another cable to Yassi Ada and placed a stern anchor. The barge would not move for the next three months.

We dived, in turn, to get the feel of the wreck. Holding my mask and mouthpiece in place with one hand, and the bottom strap of my tanks down with the other, I dropped feet first over the side of the barge with Fred. Chuck Fries looked at the second hand on his watch, gave us a thumb down signal, and noted the time in the diving log.

Everything about the dive was different from the hundred or more I had made at Cape Gelidonya. It was eerie descending into the blue depths, not being able to see the bottom at once. The wreck, itself, as it came hazily into view, lay isolated on a sloping tract of sand, with no boulders or cliffs to relieve the monotony of its environment. It was higher than anything around, a great mound of globular wine jars about fifty feet long and twenty-five feet wide. Lying across the upper end of this cargo of two-handled jars, or amphoras, was a concreted mass of iron bars, which Peter and Honor had spotted earlier as anchors. At the lower end was a depression void of amphoras, where they had found a layer of broken terracotta roof and hearth tiles; they rightly supposed this marked a galley near the ship's stern.

Far above, Chuck hammered on a crowbar hanging partly in the water, signaling us that it was time to come up.

By six o'clock the sun was low over the greying Greek islands to the west. Diving was over. Most of us jumped onto *Sanane,* which Kemal had just brought alongside, and settled down for the two-hour sail to Bodrum. Wlady and Fred remained to guard the barge, along with old "Uncle" Hasip and Genghis, two of Kemal's men.

Making Bodrum expedition headquarters had been a hard choice. Four hours a day was too long to waste in commuting. Fear of bad weather, however, kept us out of the unsheltered villages on the nearby coast of the mainland, where we might often be unable to

An unusually large group prepares a dive to clean the Byzantine wreck and attach lettered identification tags to items of cargo by means of wire stems.

land, and Yassi Ada itself swarmed with rats. Peter had told me they showed no fear of humans.

It was dark when we reached Bodrum.

For two weeks we dived without moving an object. Like scrubwomen we knelt on the cargo, cleaning seaweed from hundreds of amphoras with stiff brushes. We numbered every visible artifact with a plastic tag, each, like an artificial flower, attached by a stiff wire stem so that its numbered surface faced upward toward daylight; Herb would soon glide overhead taking photographs. Both sides of the tags were marked, but within a few weeks the indelible ink on the upper sides faded from sunlight filtered through more than a hundred feet of water.

Our work was tedious and required patience. But no detailed picture existed to show what a Byzantine ship looked like, much less the method of its construction. We wanted plans that would enable a shipwright to build a Byzantine hull plank by plank and nail by nail—and then be able to lade it. Bill Wiener was to provide this plan. If the wood was there.

Larry, in Philadelphia, had suggested measuring the wreck with a pair of plane tables, like those used by surveyors on land. I said it was impractical; a professional diver had told me they would never work under water. Now Bill had the same idea and wanted to try it.

HERB GREER

All objects on the Byzantine shipwreck were labeled with coded identification tags. The square terracotta tiles formed a firebox in the ship's galley.

He built two tables, with adjustable tripods for leveling, out of scrap lumber. Their sights, or alidades, were short lengths of rusty pipe with cross hairs fitted in. We positioned the tables on either side of the wreck and two divers began taking bearings with them on a surveying pole, moved from amphora to amphora by a third diver. The bearings, or vectors, were drawn with pencil along the bases of the sights on sheets of plastic paper attached to the tabletops. Elevation measurements were read on the surveying pole.

After a six-foot wide strip of amphoras had been plotted across the bow of the wreck, Herb photographed the area with a series of shots taken from ten feet above, to provide details for the plan Bill was piecing together. The plotted amphoras were then carried to one side of the wreck and we began the process of tagging and mapping the layer beneath. Under three layers of cargo we came to a large wooden beam. Reluctantly we stopped and covered it with sand.

At Cape Gelidonya I had learned how easily rotten planks are damaged, once uncovered, by the slightest movement of a diver, by currents, and even by fish, which dig furiously around them for worms. Now I wanted to remove as much of the cargo as possible before clearing the hull. It would be easier and safer to uncover and study the hull later, in its entirety rather than piecemeal.

The six-foot strip was only a trial trench to show us the depth of cargo, how it was stacked, and where to pay attention to possible hull remains. From it we decided we could make a major trench straight through the galley.

Plane tables had worked well for overall measurements of the wreck and for positioning its large amphoras. To use them for plotting dozens, perhaps hundreds, of small tile fragments, however, would be too time-consuming. Each diver had a total of less than forty-five minutes a day, in two dives, to work on the bottom. We were limited by the length of time we were willing to decompress at the end of each dive to avoid the bends, a crippling and often fatal divers' disease.

The bends are caused by bubbles in the blood. As a diver descends, the weight or pressure of the water on his body is prevented from crushing his air-filled lungs, sinuses, and ears by his breathing air, from a hose or tank, at a pressure equal to that of the water around him. The deeper he goes and the longer he stays, the more compressed air is absorbed into his body. To prevent this air from coming out of solution and forming bubbles in his bloodstream—like the bubbles in an uncorked bottle of champagne—he must relieve the pressure on his body slowly, by surfacing in stages according to strict schedules computed by physiologists. This is called decompressing.

We then used United States Navy diving tables, but later (1962) added a safety margin, which meant we usually hung from the shot line twenty feet below the surface for three minutes, and then for eighteen additional minutes at a depth of ten feet before the conclusion of each dive. Twenty-one minutes, twice a day, every day of the week was about all we could take of the boredom and cold. To have dived longer, especially at the deep end of the site, would have required much more decompression.

To speed excavation we lowered a new device—a mapping frame —to the seabed and positioned it over the galley area. Suggested to

A mapping frame allowed divers to record coordinates and elevations of artifacts and wood remains.

HERB GREER

us the year before by Dumas and constructed by Claude in France, it was simply a square of pipes, fifteen feet on a side, leveled with tall telescopic legs at its corners. A horizontal metal beam with wheels on its ends spanned the square, running back and forth on two sides of the frame as if on tracks. A vertical steel pole was yoked to this beam so that it could move both back and forth on the beam, and up and down. The two sides of the square frame, the beam, and the pole were all calibrated in centimeters with painted lines and numbers, like giant rulers, so that we could record the coordinates and elevation of any object on which we rested the bottom of the pole.

Work went faster now. Finds from in and around the galley area began to bring the ship to life. A large, open-mouthed water jar, similar to one we had used on *Mandalinçi*, had rolled down the slope and come to rest near a copper cooking cauldron identical to those we saw daily in Bodrum. A terracotta pipette or "wine thief," used for drawing wine from amphoras, was found close by; it reminded me of one a street vendor had used to fill my glass with lemonade in Finike.

Lamps, plates, pitchers, and cooking pots—all of baked clay— appeared as we mapped and removed the tiles. The wine pitchers were coated inside with resin to prevent them from sweating—a habit which must have started the custom of flavoring modern Greek wine with resin. One of the cooking bowls was still a quarter full of this congealed pine sap, heated during the last voyage to smear inside pitchers and amphoras.

Two dozen terracotta lamps were of the same basic type: oil was poured in through the central hole, while the hole in the nozzle held a wick.

ROBERT B. GOODMAN © NATIONAL GEOGRAPHIC SOCIETY

Our "freight elevator," a large wire basket tied to one of Dumas' old yellow lifting balloons, carried a load of pottery and tile fragments, still tagged, to the surface once or twice a day.

Sue left her aqualung on the barge and commandeered our long Bodrum dining table, to begin the painstaking job of rendering each object to scale. Her eyes proved more accurate than the rulers and calipers we used for basic measurements, her drawings more instructive than photographs. Ann swept out a stable to make our "conservation laboratory." Her hands soaked alternately in cleaning acids and mending glues, she turned countless shards into complete, and often unique, vases. She catalogued each with a detailed description to be filed with our object photographs and Sue's drawings to take back to Philadelphia. The antiquities would join those from the Bronze Age wreck in the new Bodrum Museum.

Bodrum was our home, and we took pride in our relations with its people. As foreigners we were eager to learn the language and customs of our hosts. Ann amassed an impressive "kitchen" vocabulary from morning trips to market. I felt my Turkish was becoming fluent until, much later in Ankara, I found that I really

Susan Womer commandeered the long dining table in our rented Bodrum house to use as a drawing table for recording pottery and other finds.

understood embarrassingly little. The words I knew well—hose, fathom, current, spark plug, pressure gauge, keel, sulfuric acid, angle-iron, arc-welding—didn't come up often at the cocktail party.

Most of my time in Bodrum was spent waiting in the post office, trying to make phone calls. It took hours then just to get through to Izmir. The operator turned a crank on the switchboard, shouting "Izmir, Izmir," again and again at the top of his lungs. I wondered if there really was a telephone line, or only a megaphone on the roof, which he aimed at whatever city he was calling. When the cabinet door above the switchboard swung open, I saw the inner-most workings of the system: shelves of old glass jars filled with liquid—the wet-cell batteries—formed the core of a confusing bird's nest of multicolored wires. I tried to picture a wiring diagram for it.

Karatoprak, the village closest to Yassi Ada on the mainland, had no real system, but only an unreliable, single-wire field phone for its tiny gendarmerie to call Bodrum. We used it but once.

To avoid the long trip back to Bodrum for forgotten wrenches, Kemal sailed directly to Karatoprak and telephoned for someone to bring them by jeep. Pressing the phone to his mouth, he screamed instructions to the Bodrum post office. Once. Twice. Three times. Each time louder. At last they said they understood.

Ann was in the kitchen, cleaning up with Gunay, when the message reached her. A man from the post office arrived by bicycle to say that there had been a phone call from Karatoprak and that she must go there at once. With Gunay helping translate she gathered in horror that someone had the bends. Gunay raced out to find a jeep taxi. When he returned he said he had heard that the bent diver was an American. The jeep pulled out onto the main road, lined with tearful women; perhaps they knew something that she did not— that the diver had died?

Claude alighted at that moment from the Izmir-to-Bodrum bus. Immediately he was surrounded by old men and women, sobbing, offering condolences, observing the ritual that has been all too fre-quent among families of Bodrum sponge divers.

Stones and pebbles hammered the undersides of the jeep fend-ers as the driver raced toward Karatoprak. Gunay, face grim, re-peated over and over to Ann: "Don't think, don't think." They skid-ded to a halt on the sandy waterfront. Kemal was alone, waiting for the wrenches he had requested in his obviously garbled phone call.

Years later Ann told me how much she feared the arrival of *Sanane* every night, bringing the divers home.

In two and a half months there were no more than ten calm days. The wind was furious. We had baked at Gelidonya, and now we froze from the northern blasts. Under the bright Mediterranean sun in mid-August we wore turtleneck sweaters under ski jackets, stood in the choking fumes of compressor exhaust to warm ourselves after dives, and huddled with blue lips and knees behind makeshift windbreaks. The barge, only partially sheltered by Yassi Ada, bobbed incessantly in a sea of whitecaps. Even so, most of the divers preferred sleeping on board to the long round trip to Bodrum.

We invariably arrived back in Bodrum soaking, after dark. By the time we had eaten, repaired diving equipment, printed photographs, and recorded the day's work, it was midnight or later. Ann was up at five each morning to get our five-thirty breakfast ready. We tried to sail by six. Five and a half hours' sleep is simply not enough for diving, but we continued day after day, week after week. We had no choice if the work was to progress. I learned to sleep in any position on the deck of *Sanane,* salt spray covering my clothes, my teeth rattling from the jittering planks beneath my head.

On these trips we were always wet and cold, always tired, and, more often than most would admit, a little frightened. Kemal's two sailors, wide-eyed, screaming at one another over the wind that snatched their voices away, turned back halfway to Yassi Ada the only day we sailed without him. Kemal, himself, seemed fearless.

"What's she doing in there? There's no village there," I said, pointing to a large steel-hulled freighter riding at anchor in a usually deserted cove we passed daily.

Most days were cold and windy during our first three-month excavation at Yassi Ada. The diving barge bobbed continuously in whitecaps.

"Oh, she can't come out in weather like this," Kemal laughed. We all laughed. We laughed as we sang "The Great Ship *Titanic*" against the storm.

The daily trip to Yassi Ada in the Sanane *was usually wet and uncomfortable, but we were able to discuss the day's work in advance and sometimes catch up on badly needed sleep.*

ROBERT B. GOODMAN © NATIONAL GEOGRAPHIC SOCIETY

Even when we dropped far down into watery troughs, the waves appearing to rise everywhere above us, when *Sanane*'s mast tipped so far over that it seemed impossible that it could rise again, when Kemal, himself, admitted concern to me, even then we joked and sang, at the tops of our lungs, "... when the grea-at ship went down."

Whimsy and silliness were medicine for hardship, fear, and exhaustion. We simply had no time for gravity.

Bill, skilled and dedicated to his work, played expedition clown, struggling from the barge to the wreck and back, straps loose and tank askew, weight belt somewhere down around his knees, his knife falling out of its sheath.

His job at the drafting table kept him for days at a time in Bodrum, where almost single-handedly he made the owner of the pastry shop a rich man; we were not surprised to find the shop doubled in size the next year.

Curious children followed him as he wore down the road between the excavation house and the pastry shop where he bought sticky-sweet *baklava* and *kadayif* (syrup-covered pastries), and lemonade.

"Bye bye, bye bye," the children called, testing the only English they knew.

"No, no. Bye bye, *stupid,*" Bill corrected. A delightful welcome, he thought, for the throngs of tourists who poured off a large Greek

In our Bodrum house Bill Wiener compiled data from plane tables, mapping frame, and wire grids to make an accurate plan of the ancient cargo.

ship every Friday morning for a quick look at the castle and some haggling over the prices of souvenir sponges.

Of course it backfired, and the only people ever to be greeted with Bill's salutation were our own. It became our motto. The last words a diver heard as he plunged into the waves were, more often than not, "Bye bye, stupid."

Somebody lettered a sign and nailed it to the boom mast. *Bye Bye Stupid* was now the official name of the barge.

The crew of the *Bye Bye Stupid,* mostly total strangers before they arrived in Turkey, had by now been molded into a close, efficient team.

I had been wrong about Chuck Fries. In college he had swum for Michigan, and now, without waistcoat and glasses, he was a sturdy Tarzan putting most of us, all younger, to shame; as a reaction against years in sterile hospitals, I guess, he neither shaved nor cut his hair from the moment he reached Bodrum.

Fred van Doorninck became so obsessed by the wreck that his diving partner invariably had to pull him away by his tanks at the end of each dive. Always blue with cold, his mask partly filled with blood from broken vessels in his nose, and sometimes with compressed air whistling like a boiling kettle from beneath a loose filling in his teeth, he clambered onto the barge and even before removing his tanks began talking about each new aspect of the site. His enthusiasm almost killed him. After hauling a dozen mud-filled amphoras from the wreck, he barreled to the surface to gulp fresh air, completely exhausted, unable to draw enough through his regulator to feed his starved lungs. It was minutes before we could send him down to decompress. From then, I limited the number of amphoras anyone could move on a single dive.

Sue became an expert and calm diver, able to hover effortlessly over the wreck while making drawings. Her hair grew even blonder, but her fair skin suffered badly from the intense sun. I never tan and quit trying. I kidded Bob Goodman, photographer for the *National Geographic* that he would receive any day a cable saying: Get that fat white man out of the pictures; he's ruining all the color shots.

It was during guard duty on the barge that we got to know each other best. After Jean Naz had shut down the last compressor for the night, and *Sanane* had disappeared with most of the crew, we usually sat separately for a while, grateful for the silence, lost in our own thoughts as the sky grew darker and the greying waves rolled ceaselessly beneath us. Then Uncle Hasip, his false teeth gleaming from a creased and weather-beaten face, the ever-present bottle of potent, licorice-tasting, *raki* bulging his pants pocket, would beckon us to the stern where he had fried a fresh grouper or two over a primus stove. It was after we had crawled into our sleeping bags under a great canvas flap to keep dry for the night that we talked.

The barge hardly looked like the base for a scientific expedition. Larry was by far the most meticulous of the group, insisting that every piece of metal used under water be painted with two coats of red lead and then a final coat of color. He spent hours washing and patching wet suits, keeping diving knives cleaned and greased, and grumbling all the while about some of the rest of us. I felt his dismay at "the mountain of gear piling higher and higher on the barge," which he described in a lengthy report sent back to the Main Line Diving Club. He listed in detail:

". . . regulators, tanks, neoprene rubber suits, fins, masks, snorkels, weight belts, knives, depth gauges, neoprene gloves, cotton work gloves, single-tank back packs, talcum powder, glue, tools and spare parts for regulators, and other accessories for which we had no proper storage space. Heavy equipment included three high-pressure compressors for filling tanks, a three-ton road compressor that ran the air lift, two electric generators, a portable recompression chamber in a crate, large-volume compressed air storage tanks, fifty-five-gallon oil drums and assorted GI cans of fuel, cable, anchor chain, hawsers, rope, and other matériel. Plus a British Sea Gull outboard motor, surplus army footlockers for stowing regulators, coils of diving hose and coils of heavy duty wire for underwater lights, tool chest, maintenance tools and spare parts for the machinery, hand pump and funnels for fueling compressors. Special gear for underwater sketching and measuring included aluminum clipboards, plastic sheets for drawing, boxes of solid graphite pencils, small carpenters' levels, meter sticks, measuring tapes, plumb lines, and more. For photography there were one Leica with underwater housing and flash, two Roleimarin underwater cameras with flash, one Hasselblad with custom plastic underwater housing, two Pathé Ciné 16mm movie cameras with underwater housing, one Fenjohn custom 16mm underwater movie camera, underwater light meters, and, for surface and journalistic work, a morass of cameras including Leicas, Hasselblads, Cannons, and Nikons, all supported by crates of flashbulbs, tripods, cartons of 36-exposure films, extensive inventory of lenses, timers, view finders, cable releases, and what have you. Also lifting balloons, large air-lift pipes, frames and pipes for bottom, and air-lift hose. Other assorted junk and equipment littering the deck of the barge included buckets, personal dive equipment bags, several water jars, cook stove and pots and pans, baskets, wire screen, tarpaulins, canvas and spring cots, spear gun, old mattresses, sleeping bags and blankets, equipment trunks, clothesline with drying bathing suits and rubber wet suits, old books and magazines, heavy shackles and other boat equipment, coils of light lines, surplus army field jackets, watermelons, dirty clothes, rusty nails, extra weight packs, cans of grease, an assortment of wire brushes, heavy tools such as sledge and bars, winch handle, dead fish (for the frying pan), wood blocks, an occasional very dirty towel, well-used copies of the *Navy Diving Manual,* and just about everything imaginable, including a population of rats which became increasingly bold toward the end of the season, venturing forth from the barge hold to run skittering across one's feet. All this and sixteen or seventeen people on one barge whose deck surface was old splintering wood partly covered by the remains of previous loads of concrete and gravel, with oil, tar and grease spots, and a sporting variety of broken and rusty nail heads and spikes . . . but our feet were so toughened that we went barefoot for weeks in this environment without complaint."

The divers who spent the night on the barge usually tried to get off a dive as soon as they saw *Sanane* appear on the morning horizon. No dives were to be made earlier, for we wanted reliable transportation in case of emergency.

Wlady and Eric had just come up when we bumped alongside and scrambled onto the rolling barge. Wlady had a huge grin. He opened an old film canister and lifted out a wad of cotton. Inside a tiny gold coin gleamed as if new.

The profile of a young man with ribbons tied around his head and cloak over his shoulder was stamped in the center of the coin. Around the edge, in raised letters, was his name:

"Heraclius! At last we can date the wreck! It's early seventh century!"

To be honest, that is not exactly what was said. There was not a numismatist among us. As closely as I can recall, what actually was said as we crowded around Wlady was:

"Hey, look at that!"

"Whatta ya think it says?"

"Lemme see!"

"Wow!"

"You think it's Coptic?"

"I dunno."

"Move a minute."

The coin, the first of sixteen gold and more than fifty copper coins, eventually allowed us to date the wreck to the middle years of the Emperor Heraclius, who reigned between A.D. 610 and 641.

Heraclius ruled at a difficult time. He had been called from Africa to take over a faltering Byzantine empire. So fiercely was he pressed by attacking Persian armies that at first he considered moving the capital of the empire from Constantinople to Carthage. When he finally drove the Persians back and secured his eastern frontier, a new threat arose. The Arabs, bursting forth under the inspiration of their leader Mohammed, were soon annexing Syria, Palestine, and Egypt. Heraclius and his empire were too worn down to defend these possessions longer. Much of his remaining life was spent in religious meditation.

The coin was the first in a deluge of small objects. Even more precise surveying methods were needed. We made squares of angle-iron, from two to six feet on a side, strung them like tennis rackets with heavy wire, and scattered them on the wreck. Hovering over these grids, the sheets of plastic paper attached to our clipboards inked with similar grids at one-tenth scale, we made accurate

Sixteen gold coins gave an approximate date for the sinking of the Byzantine ship, but copper coins narrowed this to almost precisely A.D. 625.

drawings of the areas beneath. We keyed the corners of the grids onto Bill's plan with the plane tables and mapping frame.

We lowered our air-lift pipe in sections, assembled it on the bottom, and anchored it in the middle of the galley area; its upper end was buoyed sixty feet above by an oil-drum float. No matter how carefully we vacuumed the sand, with two divers working together, there was always the chance that we might inadvertently suck up a small object and lose it out of the top. Claude designed a wire basket and bolted it to the top of the pipe. The mesh of the wires allowed fine sand and mud to be carried away by the current, but

Larry Joline prepares to take an elevation measurement by noting the distance between an amphora and the horizontal grid wires above it.

HERB GREER

larger particles and small objects from the galley were funneled down into a cloth bag tied below the basket.

Whenever the bag was full we raised it to the barge by rope and emptied it on deck. We spent hours searching through the muck of broken shells and mud, hoping not to find anything since we would never know its original position on the wreck. But one by one a few objects did appear, miraculously unbroken by their accidental trip through the pipe: pottery fragments, lead weights, glass, another gold coin, the missing half of a lamp found earlier.

The smell of autumn, even across the waves, was strong in the air when we began to uncover the wood in the galley area. Chuck Fries and David Owen had to return to America. The rest of us decided to stay on for a few more weeks, even without a doctor.

Then the newspaper article appeared.

It said that George Bass was not really an archaeologist but an international smuggler, that the members of his staff at Yassi Ada were not students but smugglers, and that several had been arrested for clandestine excavation of tombs near Bodrum. It ended with an ominous statement that the proper authorities were stopping the expedition.

Who would write such a thing, and why? Our commissioner had just taken ill and had left Bodrum, and his replacement had not yet arrived. There was no other official to whom I could turn, for Yüksel Eğdemir, serving as assistant commissioner, was also out of town. I had to get to Ankara by the fastest possible means to straighten the matter out.

I'm scared to death of airplanes. I had even extended my army tour in Korea by more than a month and spent seventeen days as sanitation officer on a troopship rather than fly back across the Pacific; I missed the chance to work on an important dig that summer. Out of my first forty years I spent well over half a year on ships in twenty-seven Atlantic crossings.

Wlady drove me to the Izmir airport in his minibus.

"I can't do it, Wlady, I can't."

"Okay, I'll buy the ticket."

"No, I can't."

"How about if I go with you?"

Wlady bought two tickets and we boarded the plane. Of course I couldn't let go of the arm rests, so he finished his lunch from the tray on his lap and then finished mine. It was bumpy over the mountains, which was bad enough, but when we suddenly started to descend in circles right in the middle of nowhere I was sure something was wrong.

"This isn't Ankara, is it?"

"No."

"I knew it. We must be making a crash landing."

It was a scheduled stop at Afyon we didn't know about. We got off and stretched our legs in the small terminal. Soon it was time to go, but taking off once in a year, much less in a day, was my limit.

"You go ahead, Wlady, I'll get there by myself."

Passengers reboarded the plane. The stewardess asked me if I was coming. No. The pilot came back and asked me if I was ready. "No, no. I've just met some old friends in the airport and I'm staying with them." I took a taxi the remaining two hundred miles to Ankara.

The question of our work being stopped was quickly answered next morning. I didn't even have to go to the Department of Antiquities, but first called on an old friend, Raci Temizer, director of the remarkable Hittite Museum in Ankara, for advice.

"Don't pay any attention to this newspaper," he said on reading the clipping. "Nobody does."

We hired a car to Izmir, where we changed to Wlady's minibus. It was after dark the next day when we got back to Bodrum. Dusty and parched from the long, hot drive, we stopped at the pastry shop for a cold lemonade. Eric and Herb found us there.

"We have some bad news. Really bad news." There was a pause. "Larry's bent."

"When? Where is he?"

Eric supplied the details as we ran toward the waterfront customs house.

"It was his first dive of the morning . . . He was diving at one hundred fifteen feet with one hundred thirty-foot tables. He came up on time and his ascent was perfectly timed . . ."

Larry thought he had a stomach cramp at the decompression stop. On the barge the cramps got worse, and Kemal, no stranger to the bends, recognized what was happening before anyone else.

The cure for the bends is to put the diver back under pressure, in a steel chamber, to squeeze the bubbles down in size; the sponge

Larry Joline collapses from the bends on the deck of the barge, but is supported by Yüksel Eğdemir, Eric Ryan (behind), and Claude Duthuit.

divers' remedy, to send the stricken diver back down under water, is uncertain and dangerous, especially as the diver is liable to lose consciousness.

Although there was a portable chamber crated on the barge—Larry had urged me all summer to have it out and ready—the team decided to rush him to the Turkish navy's large recompression chamber in Istanbul. By the time *Sanane* reached Bodrum, however, Larry was paralyzed from the waist down. He needed immediate recompression.

Claude remembered the portable chamber that Peter Throckmorton had left in Bodrum customs the year before—the chamber we had hoped to use at Cape Gelidonya—and thought it might still be there. They found it in a warehouse, still crated. A sponge-boat captain volunteered to provide air with his 1909 vintage one-lung compressor. Mahmout, the town mechanic, hurriedly turned metal fittings on his lathe for the attachments, and a thick diver's hose was run across the quay from the boat into the customs house.

By the time I arrived a crowd had gathered. Little boys strained to get a glimpse of what was going on as opportunistic vendors hawked peanuts and *gazoz*. I saw Tosun Sezen and Baskin Sokullu, two of the best divers in Turkey, sitting by the chamber controls. Larry looked out of the small round window of the chamber and gave a smile. His was the only smiling face.

The chamber was the size of a coffin. Its nearly cylindrical shape tapered toward his feet since it had been pulled out of several telescoping sections. It was good for treating only minor cases of the bends, and its thin walls were not built to withstand the pressures needed for treating a case as serious as Larry's. Once committed to a treatment schedule, however, he had to stick it out although he was getting no better. In fact, the notes he held to the window told us that he was getting worse. He needed the treatment that only the large chamber in Istanbul could offer.

Larry was treated in a recompression chamber in Bo-
drum before being flown to Istanbul. Baskin Sokullu
and Tosun Sezen tend him, with Jo Sezen.

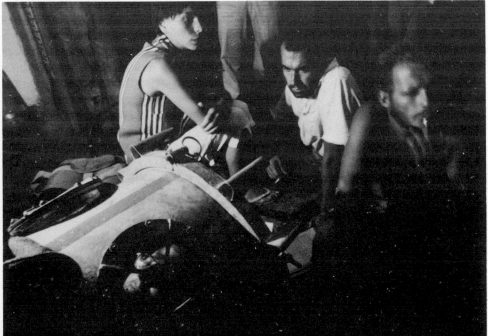

It was a situation we had talked about, again and again, but our plans were far from perfect. We were too isolated. Ideally, the diver should be transported in a portable chamber to a larger one. A Turkish army helicopter, offered earlier in the summer, had been ruled out; leaving the diver in a chamber slung beneath a "chopper" would mean leaving him unattended during the flight. Trucks had been considered, but none of us would have risked being battered to pieces inside a small chamber on the nearly impassable road to Izmir; a new highway was under construction and detours led over mountains and through stream beds. We even feared that a collapsible portable chamber might spring a leak in a joint, causing nearly instant death from the pressure drop. There were no seaplanes in the area. Boats are too slow.

Our best plan was our only plan: get the diver to Istanbul as fast as possible, even though not under pressure during the trip.

Eric and Claude had already called the American consulate in Izmir and asked for help. A light United States army plane would be ready to take off at five in the morning with a flight plan that would keep it low over the sea all the way; in the unpressurized cockpit, Larry would have gotten worse during a normal flight path over the mountains.

There are cases of divers going berserk and battering their heads bloody inside one-man chambers. With air screaming in and out next to his head, nearly unable to move, suffering intense heat and then cold as pressure was added and then let slowly drop, not knowing the condition of the rubber gaskets on which his life depended, Larry remained calm throughout.

After seven hours he was pulled from the "coffin." Supported on both sides, his feet dragging behind him, he was taken to Wlady's minibus. Neither Wlady nor I was in condition to drive, having driven through the previous night, but Claude was ready; I knew from driving in Paris traffic with him that he would lose no time in getting Larry to Izmir.

Larry looked at me. "I'm sorry, George."

He was sorry.

"Don't let him fall asleep!" Kemal shouted after the minibus. Inside, Eric and others massaged Larry's legs on the back seat. At Seljuk they roused him to get out, but he couldn't urinate; it was a bad sign.

The airfield in Izmir was deserted when they arrived, and they walked him back and forth, between them, on the asphalt. A light plane landed about half an hour later, just as the consulate car drove up. Larry was lifted into the cockpit, and an oxygen mask strapped to his face.

Eric and Claude didn't know if they would see him again. Or if he would be confined to a wheelchair the rest of his life. What could they say? They grinned and called out simultaneously:

"Bye bye, Stupid!"

In Bodrum a drained, empty feeling replaced the rush of adrenaline in our bodies once Larry had gone. By mutual instinct we drifted to the harbor cafe, first to sit and then to talk. Finally I asked the question:

"Shall we go on or not? I won't think anybody is chicken if you don't want to dive any more."

Sue Womer answered for the group, quietly.

"It's no more dangerous now than it has been all summer. I want to keep on."

It was all that was ever said about it.

We hung around Bodrum next day, waiting for the telephone call which came that night.

"He's all right. He'll be in the chamber for thirty-eight hours, but he's O.K."

Larry was in the hospital for two weeks before he rejoined us, and limped for months afterward. Even today, when he is tired, I see the limp return.

As work continued at Yassi Ada we came to know more about the crew who manned its doomed ship. A yellow glass pendant molded with a cruciform monogram of the name Theodore appeared in the air-lift bag. From the sand under the roof tiles we dug more lamps, coins, and eating wares. One night, as we delicately chipped concretion from the captain's steelyard beam used for weighing heavy cargo, we came upon his name, punched awkwardly in Greek letters: George Senior Sea-Captain. The counterpoise for the steelyard was a lead-filled bronze bust of helmeted Athena, immediately recognized by the Gorgon's head on her breastplate. But Captain George did not worship a pagan goddess. He was a devout Christian, as the crosses carved beside his name attest; a bronze censer and cross lay near the steelyard. A second, smaller steelyard with

The counterweight for the Byzantine ship's main balance was a lead-filled bronze bust of Athena, identified by the Gorgon's head on her breast.

A bronze censer may have provided incense after meals or been used for sanctifying the ship.

chains, hooks, and pear-shaped lead counterpoise was further evidence of his business needs. The mercantile and religious natures of a merchant of the period were united on a set of disc-shaped bronze weights, each inlaid with a silver cross above the Greek figure denoting the number of ounces.

Poseidon tells us when to quit. The first autumn storm swooped down on the barge at night, wrenching her exhausted anchors from the sand and rock they had clutched so stubbornly through the summer's unceasing *meltem*. It was a year to the day since we were washed from our camp at Cape Gelidonya.

Next morning *Sanane* was defeated, for the first time with Kemal at her helm, and turned back halfway to Yassi Ada, fleeing before packs of waves that gave chase with open, foam-flecked jaws. We took to the jeep. From Bodrum I drove with Kemal to the mountains opposite the island, and with field glasses searched out the barge and our companions who stood guard on her deck. She had not yet drifted far, but she looked tiny and vulnerable in a vast sea.

Next day, after a worried, sleepless night punctuated by banging shutters and splintering panes of glass, we sailed again. At first we did not see her. Then she came into view, not far from Yassi Ada, a sodden shambles of shattered cots, parted lines, and shredded canvas. Her crew greeted us, cold and tired.

We dived to see what had kept the barge from being swept away into the Aegean. We traced the furrow plowed by the largest anchor as it was dragged over the seabed, and found the anchor scarcely clinging by the peak of one fluke to another of Yassi Ada's victims, a wreck of the Late Roman period.

With our last dives we covered the Byzantine remains with rubberized cloth weighted down with sand and stones, hoping it would protect them from currents and curious divers.

CHAPTER VI
Bottom Time

~~~~~~
~~~~~~
~~~~~~

WE MOVED to Yassi Ada in 1962, to stop wasting four hours a day commuting from Bodrum. Claude had earlier visited a Paris exterminating firm to learn what could be done about the rats that infest the island.

"What do these rats eat?" the diminutive, elderly lady asked him.

"There's scrub brush and thistles. Maybe an occasional sea gull egg."

"I see. And what do they drink?"

"There's no fresh water."

Then, politely, "What do these rats look like?"

"I haven't seen one myself," Claude admitted.

"You must be mistaken. There can be no rats there."

But there are rats. By the hundreds . . . or thousands. How they survive on the nearly barren rock remains a mystery, but I have no doubts as to their origins:

Between Yassi Ada and the mainland lie larger, greener islands, one with a copious spring. There are no rats there. Nor is there a reef. Nor wrecks. Are our rats descended from Greek, Roman, or Byzantine castaways, or are they a chronologically mixed breed of shipwrecked rodents?

We decided to give the rats free run of the island and built a cage of concrete, stone, nylon screen, and canvas for the men divers; a few relatively rodent-proof tents housed the women divers and couples. Below, on the water's edge, we sledged out a flat beach for a smaller cage—our kitchen—and a dining table; from the beach we constructed a jetty for boats out of boulders capped with concrete.

In the sea, mapping the hull remains of the Byzantine ship presented our greatest problem: an exact plan of the fragmentary wood required more accurate methods than any previously used under water. Over countless cups of coffee during the preceding winter, Larry and I had reached a possible solution.

Experience had shown that photographing was quicker than

A diver uses one of two photo towers supported on the scaffolding of angle-iron frames erected over the Byzantine wreck. One of the plane tables used to position the step-frames is seen in the upper right hand corner. Amphoras already removed from the cargo by excavators line the sides of the site.

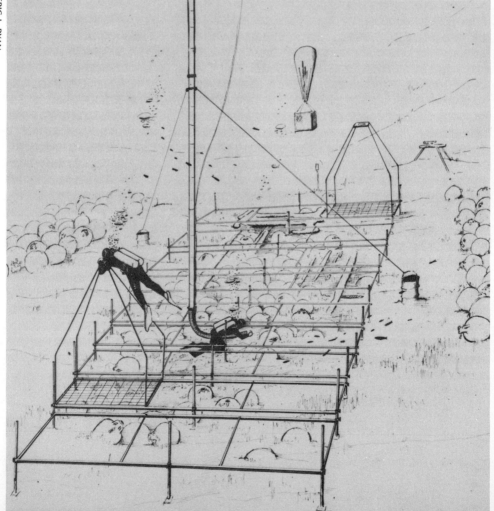

drawing under water, but was less controlled, less accurate for mapping. To add control we designed a scaffolding of nine angle-iron frames, simple rectangles eighteen feet long and six feet wide, supported on pipe legs. Assembled and leveled over the site, the scaffolding formed nine horizontal steps running up the slope on which the wreck lay, each step placed as close to the seabed as possible. Metal plates under the pipe legs prevented them from settling far into the sand, but constant checks with a carpenter's level on the steps were still necessary.

We lowered two photographic towers of light metal, four-legged spiders fifteen feet tall. The square base of each was gridded with tightly stretched elastic cords eight inches apart; the bases fit perfectly over the three equal squares into which each frame was divided by wooden strips. Thus, by sliding the towers over the frames as if on tracks, we could return again and again to twenty-seven permanent positions for photography. Holes in the tops of the towers held our Rolleimarin camera in a vertical position. Because camera settings for distance and light level seldom varied, any diver could now take perfect grid photographs with minimal photographic ability.

The resultant pictures could not be glued together to form a map, nor could they be copied directly onto our expanding plan of the site. Each grid photo was first traced onto paper, where corrections were made for scale (objects higher on the slope appeared larger than those lower down and farther from the camera), distortion caused by the difference between the index of refraction of water and that of the air in the camera (which makes a drinking straw half in water seem bent if viewed from the side of a glass tumbler), and parallax (only objects directly below the camera appeared in true relation to the grid wires above them).

Fred, who quietly and on his own initiative had assumed responsibility for mapping the hull, was delighted with the results. He found our corrected grid pictures matched so closely on the plan that there was seldom an error of more than a pencil line's thickness along the edge of a timber carried from one grid drawing to another.

As we gently uncovered the timbers, fanning sand into great mounds to be sucked away with the air lift, we encountered an unexpected problem. The ship, unlike copper-fastened ships of earlier Greco-Roman times, had been built with iron nails, which had rusted away years ago. The slightest movement by a diver shifted

Horizontal steps running up the slope provide level bases for photo towers. The air lift is buoyed at its top by an air-filled oil drum and anchored by wires running to rock-filled oil drums. The air-lift basket funnels objects into the catch-bag below.

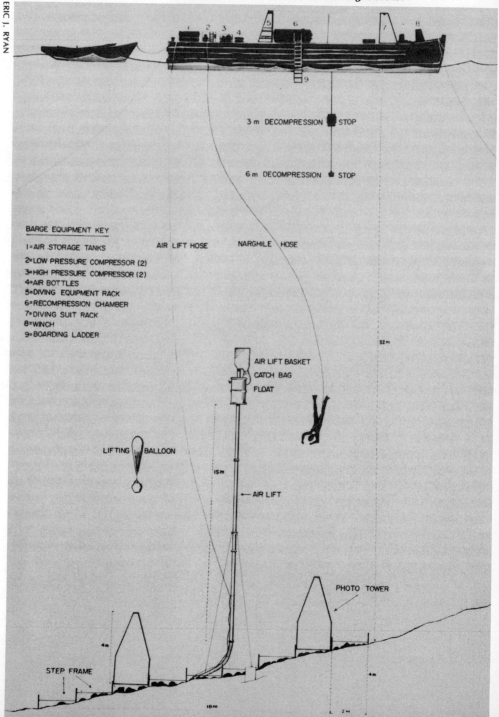

ERIC J. RYAN

3 m DECOMPRESSION STOP

6 m DECOMPRESSION STOP

AIR LIFT HOSE   NARGHILE HOSE

BARGE EQUIPMENT KEY

1 = AIR STORAGE TANKS
2 = LOW PRESSURE COMPRESSOR (2)
3 = HIGH PRESSURE COMPRESSOR (2)
4 = AIR BOTTLES
5 = DIVING EQUIPMENT RACK
6 = RECOMPRESSION CHAMBER
7 = DIVING SUIT RACK
8 = WINCH
9 = BOARDING LADDER

32 m

AIR LIFT BASKET
CATCH BAG
FLOAT

LIFTING BALLOON

15 m

— AIR LIFT

PHOTO TOWER

4 m

4 m

STEP FRAME

18 m

2 m

pieces of wood from their resting place of thirteen centuries. We worked without fins, a dangerous practice since discontinued, our heads hanging down from the metal frames on which our heavily weighted bodies rested. Still, currents and even fish disturbed the disconnected wooden remains before their positions were accurately plotted.

"Where can we find a lot of knitting needles?" I had to use an English–Turkish dictionary to ask Mustafa Kapkin the question.

Mustafa couldn't answer, but he countered by suggesting bicycle spokes when I explained what I had in mind.

We found a hundred, then two hundred, and eventually located more than two thousand bicycle spokes by scouring shops between Bodrum and Izmir. We sharpened the tip of each on a grindstone, bent the opposite end over to form a head, and shoved them through waterlogged wood, pinning each fragment to the seabed until much of the preserved hull, slowly stripped of its blanket of sand, lay like a giant butterfly pinned to a piece of cardboard. Then, almost at leisure, we mapped it from the photo towers.

Larry never used the techniques he had helped to invent. Advised against deep diving after his case of bends, he turned his considerable talents to land-based jobs. He taught newcomers to dive, sometimes first how to swim more effectively. He kept excavation records with meticulous care, dogging divers from the dining table to their beds, a determined inquisitor with notebook and pencil. At least once a week he sailed to the smithies of Bodrum.

Larry had arrived that summer earlier than the rest of the staff and, through necessity, had learned more Turkish than most. He could ably direct the blacksmiths who transformed chunks of scrap metal into the "scientific" equipment we needed, and a lasting, mutual respect grew between them; he was the only one of us to earn the affectionate sobriquet *amca,* "uncle," in Bodrum.

For work requiring power tools he went to Mahmout, a machinist so skilled he was able to recondition a pair of British warship engines, salvaged after nearly twenty years on the seabed, to power two new Bodrum trawlers. For rougher fittings—the endless fodder of shackles, rings, ladder rungs, chain, and buoys the expedition consumed—Larry turned to simpler shops. I never knew which one to find him in when I came to town.

"There you are, Larry *amca. Merhaba,* Basri."

Larry sat on a chair at the edge of blacksmith Basri's dirt-floored workshop. He knew that if he left, a farmer with broken plow or captain needing links of chain would quickly take his place, and our work would be laid aside. Basri put down his tools only long enough to offer a cigarette from a crushed packet, and to ask how I wanted my Turkish coffee: plain, medium, or sweet.

A young apprentice, face blackened with soot, stared blankly at the ceiling as with both hands he opened and closed the worn wooden handles of an ancient bellows behind Basri's furnace. With each slow puff of air the coals around a hunk of iron turned bright red and cooled to black again. With a hissing wet brush of twigs Basri shifted the coals until the iron glowed with its own light. When it was ready he grabbed it with tongs and placed it on the anvil. In a silent drill timed by years of practice, though he looked no more than ten, the boy left his post at the bellows and took up a huge hammer. As the blacksmith turned the quickly cooling iron with one hand on the tongs, he and the boy hammered it into a new shape with an unbroken rhythm of alternating blows. When the metal had darkened, the blacksmith tossed it sizzling into a rusty oil drum of dirty water. The boy took his place again behind the bellows. No word had been spoken.

Larry's bends caused changes in the divers' routine as well as his own. We scheduled dives with a greater margin for safety than ever, pretending, when reading decompression tables, that we were diving deeper and longer than we actually were. We shut off the electric generators at 10:00 P.M. to encourage sleep. We also instituted prohibition six days a week, although alcohol had played no part in Larry's accident. A single bottle of beer the night before diving, we learned on good authority, can increase a diver's susceptibility to the bends.

On Fridays we did not dive. Friday was market day in Bodrum, the day to replenish supplies, and that became our day of rest. Thursday night became party night.

We made pathetic attempts to get especially clean then, showering with single cups of precious fresh water brought to the island in fifty-five-gallon oil drums for drinking, washing, cooking, and the darkroom. Men crowded around the canvas water bag to shave while women rinsed salt from their hair.

Our cooks rose to the occasion, voluntarily bringing hors d'oeuvres of fried potatoes, white cheese, peanuts, and black olives up to the cage from the beach. Eric appointed himself social chairman, mixing cocktails of whatever was available on a rough bar of packing crates. His choice was usually limited to vodka and lemonade or raki and tepid water, but he served them with flair.

The dull beating on an oil drum serving as a dinner bell ended the cocktail hour. We trooped single file down steps carved out of the island to a special meal of chicken or shish kebab on the beach, and then trooped back up again.

The cage was a simple shelter fifty feet long and fifteen feet wide, with concrete floor, a stone wall on the north side and west end to block out the cold *meltem,* nylon screen around the other sides to keep out vermin, and a roof of surplus canvas that flapped incessantly in the wind, snapping against its supporting rafters. Fifteen army cots lined the sides at night, but were pushed together by day to make room for machine shop, drafting area, photo studio, business office, and conservation laboratory. On party nights we lounged over the cots, singing by flickering kerosene lamps as Claude, Eric, and Susan took turns on the guitar. It was often nearly morning before the last strains of our off-key sea chanties drifted over the water and conversation ended.

We had become far more than an efficient team. We had become fast friends. For many of us our closest friendships were forged there. During months away from Yassi Ada, no holiday or conference passed without drawing half a dozen of us together from different parts of the country for a weekend reunion.

The parties were a release from the relentless pressure of the week. Bottom time had become an obsession. I wanted divers continuously on the wreck as long as there was enough light to work by.

To increase our daily excavating time, we used hookah, or *narghile,* the technique of supplying air to divers from a surface compressor via hoses so that we were no longer limited in time by the air in the tanks on our backs. Both compressors and hoses were far more reliable than those we were forced to use at Cape Gelidonya.

We began as early as possible each morning, the lengths of afternoon dives being dependent on the interval between morning and afternoon dives; even on the surface, a diver continues to exhale surplus nitrogen for hours after a dive. Following consultation with Fred about the day's priorities, I read a schedule of seven or eight two-man teams at breakfast, instructing each which square of the scaffolding to work in, and then passed the list to Claude to implement:

1. George and David, clean area 9A for photography
2. Jack and Wlady, photograph 9A, remove amphoras in 9B
3. Doc and Fred, remove all tagged objects in 9C
4. Oktay and Agnes, air-lift in 9B
5. Oguz and André, continue air-lifting in 9B
6. Eric and Önder, tag all uncovered objects in 9B
7. Claude and Susan, air-lift in area 3B

When the sun was high enough to light the wreck, we rowed the one hundred fifty yards from beach to barge. Teams were scheduled so as to be always diving, decompressing, getting suited, tending hose, or serving as back-up to the tenders—helping coil and uncoil hoses, and keeping a constant watch on fuel levels and pressure in the compressors. Each day one of us acted as timekeeper, another as barge chief; the latter's duties included starting and stopping compressors, checking the one-man recompression chamber we now had on board, fueling engines, inspecting hoses and anchor cables, pumping out bilge water, and yelling at divers to hang up their rubber suits instead of strewing them over the deck. In case of emergency I wanted each team member thoroughly familiar with every job on the barge, although David Owen, whose esoteric study of ancient Near Eastern languages belied an uncommonly practical nature, was mainly responsible for keeping a dozen machines running through the summer.

Seldom did more than a couple of minutes pass between dives.

"O.K. Let's go," Claude called, "they're at the twenty-foot stop."

Oktay and Agnes, already suited, rinsed their masks and moved to the edge of the barge. Agnes' father, Doctor Beauvy, and Fred moved up to the ten-foot decompression stop, removed their hookah harnesses, and signaled their tenders, Oguz Alpözen and André Morel, to pull up their hoses; an independent air supply was kept at the stop to allow divers to finish decompressing without holding up the next team who needed their hoses and regulators.

Oguz and André immediately began to dress for their dive, replaced as hose tenders by Eric and Önder Seren, who strapped the harnesses onto Oktay and Agnes. Before they had finished, a camel bell jangled loudly close by. Claude answered the "telephone," hauling in a clipboard that hung by a string to the ten-foot decompression stop.

"Fred says they didn't get all the tagged objects out of 9C," he relayed the written message.

"Finish that up first, then," I told Agnes as they went over the side. Not a minute had been wasted between dives. With time out only for lunch and a brief siesta, the routine would continue until sunset.

Although we were visited the following winter by navy and civilian divers to learn our mapping methods, we still were not satisfied with them. They still required too much bottom time.

In 1960, at Cape Gelidonya, Claude had suggested that we try aerial survey techniques, a suggestion seconded by Bill Wiener in 1961. I couldn't understand what they were talking about: "operators draw a map by floating a dot of light on the surface of a projected three-dimensional picture by turning wheels while looking through glasses with red and green lenses." Still, it seemed worth investigating for the 1963 campaign. I wrote to one of the largest aerial survey firms in the world, and to one of the biggest cartographic departments in America, asking each how to make aerial surveys; I had, at that time, only a vague idea that planes flew over the surface of the earth taking stereophotographs of features below, and that somehow from these pictures contour maps showing mountains, valleys, ridges, and plateaus were made. In each letter I made a basic error. I said that we wanted to use the technique to map ancient shipwrecks. The answers were nearly identical, one being more detailed than the other: it was impossible to do underwater photogrammetry (the art of making maps from stereophotographs) they said, there were too many complex problems, the navy had tried and given up. I wrote back to each that I hadn't asked how to do it under water, but how to do it at all, saying that we were a group of archaeologists who just happened to be working on the seabed, and had found that most things that one could do on land could be duplicated fairly easily under water. Neither replied.

Professor Harold Edgerton of MIT, inventor of the stroboscopic flash and frequent colleague of Cousteau, was the first person I talked to who saw no great problem. He suggested we might mount two identical cameras on a bar to take the needed stereo pairs. I was too embarrassed to tell him we couldn't afford two cameras. I wondered if one camera might work as well if moved from place to place, imitating the flight of an airplane. I imagined a horizontal bar floated above the wreck, held up by two submerged buoys, with a camera slid along its length, always pointing down. We would take pictures at point A, then point B, then C, etc., and the photos taken at A and B would be a stereo pair, those at B and C another, and so on.

In order to take stereophotographs, a diver moves his camera along a metal bar floated horizontally above the wreck. Notches cut into the bar indicate the position from which each photograph is taken, and the camera is carefully balanced to hang vertically from gimbals.

ERIC J. RYAN

I met Julian Whittlesey, an architect involved in city planning in India and elsewhere, who was familiar with aerial survey techniques and had worked as an archaeological architect some years before in Athens. He was fascinated by our ideas and volunteered to join us, to work out technical details.

At about the same time I met a chubby, slightly balding young man with horn-rimmed glasses like my own. Ever since, Donald Rosencrantz and I have been mistaken for brothers, twins, or even one another. Don was ready to leave his job as a chemist for Eastman Kodak for the chance to join an underwater expedition. As with many of the mainstays of our staff, I simply wasn't interested at first; I suppose that subconsciously, even though I knew better, I still sought strapping, robust athletes, strong of jaw and thick of hair, a picture few of us matched. Eric sat through my interview with Don. When I voiced doubts afterward, Eric encouraged me to reconsider: "He wants to go so bad."

Don helped immensely with the stereophotogrammetry program in 1963; his knowledge of films and developers enabled him to obtain what a noted authority on marine science called the clearest underwater photographs he had seen. Eventually Don became our major adviser in all technical areas. Ironically, under the pounds he shed each diving season he probably had more muscle than any member of the group.

The new mapping system showed great promise that summer. Knowing the focal length of the camera, and the distance between points on the bar from which pictures were taken, Julian calculated the distance between the camera and objects photographed, after measuring slight differences on the photographs with a micrometer. For the first time we were able to make three-dimensional plans

Julian Whittlesey measures parallax with a micrometer while viewing the Byzantine wreck in three dimensions through a stereoscope on Yassi Ada.

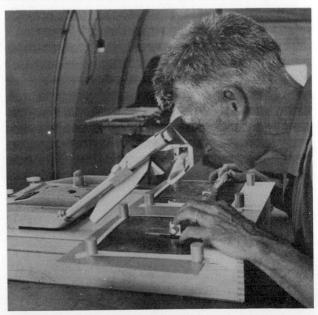

without spending hours on the seabed taking hundreds of elevation measurements by hand with a plumb bob.

Eric made a sketch of the "floating bar" system over the site. I sent a copy to the cartography department, which had told us underwater photogrammetry was impossible, and received in return a two-page explanation of why our method could not possibly work. Meanwhile we continued to get excellent results.

Even with the hull fragments mapped on the seabed, Fred needed to study them individually on land, to determine the position of every score line, the angle of every nail hole. We tried hauling them up as slowly as possible, but even when shrouded in protective cloth sheets the fragile timbers suffered badly from movement. Fred returned from a Bodrum blacksmith shop with an improvised wire basket nearly twenty feet long and a foot square. He lowered it

Like submarine pallbearers, a team of divers carries a basket of wooden hull remains from the shipwreck up the slope to Yassi Ada.

MUSTAFA KAPKIN

almost daily onto the wreck and, with three companions, placed bits of timbers inside. Then, wearing tennis shoes instead of fins, they carried it gently in long gliding steps up the slope to the island, 450 feet north and 120 feet up. The wood was placed immediately into water tanks built on the beach to prevent its warping and shrinking out of recognition. Although the wood was kept wet for several years thereafter in Bodrum, there was no scientific need to preserve it once Fred had drawn and photographed each piece in minute detail; it was far too fragmentary to warrant the expenditure of time and money for chemical treatment.

Some of the material we mapped and raised over the years we did not yet fully understand. This included over 150 concretions that had formed around iron objects soon after the ship settled to the bottom. Although virtually all traces of iron had disappeared

David Owen and Fred van Doorninck walk ashore with a basket of wood remains, supported by Peter Fries and Oguz Alpözen. Kemal Aras wades over to help.

from them, each concretion retained a perfect mold of the original iron implement inside. We could not guess what the original objects were from the external appearances of the concretions, but we had carefully plotted the position of each in the wreck.

The ability to cast replicas of disintegrated iron objects by cutting concretions into open sections, washing out the small amounts of iron oxide, or rust, and filling the resultant molds with plaster was already well known to marine archaeologists. The brittle nature and stark appearance of plaster of paris made it a poor casting material, however, especially for extremely thin objects. Larry experimented with a number of substitutes and learned that best results were obtained from polysulphide rubber compounds. Not only did casts with this material preserve the finest details of the molds, but they also attracted a thin surface layer of iron oxide from the molds, giving them the appearance of actual, though slightly

Using tags still attached to wood fragments and photographs of the same pieces on the seabed, Fred van Doorninck reassembles a plank.

A mass of concreted anchors is lifted from the water. The concretions are nearly hollow, the iron having rusted away long ago.

Few iron objects could be identified by the amorphous concretions that formed over them. An x-ray here reveals the cavity left by a nail.

rusty, iron objects. Larry had also brought an electric rotary saw with diamond-edged blades. Still, the time needed to saw open concretions, prepare cardboard shims to compensate for the amount of concretion destroyed by the thickness of the saw blade, then cast the material, and, finally, break away the concretion from the cast, meant that little progress was made in 1963.

A multitude of other objects—coins, lamps, weights, fishing tackle, glass, tableware, and cooking pots—continued to flow from the wreck. Ann was occupied with cataloguing them and mending terracotta tile fragments. By the fall of 1963 we had a mountain of material on hand. There was little left to do on the sea floor but to pull up a few last pieces before beginning the job of trying to make sense of it all.

Ann Bass mends tiles from the roof of the Byzantine ship's galley. These fragments provided the first certain knowledge of such roofing in antiquity.

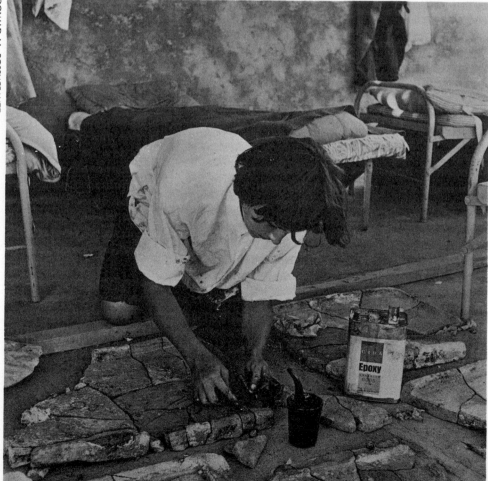

DONALD M. ROSENCRANTZ

CHAPTER VII
The *Asherah*

~~~~~~

THE siren who first drew Peter into the sea near Bodrum sang also to me. I had seen her photograph in
Peter's New York loft the night we met. A beautiful,
veiled woman of bronze, she had been fished up somewhere off the
southern coast of Turkey in the early 1950s. Peter, hearing of her in
Istanbul, had trekked southward in quest of the wreck that gave her
up; perhaps she represented an entire cargo of art works like that
found off Greek Antikythera in 1901. He learned that she came from
a depth of three hundred feet, far too deep for ordinary diving
equipment. Sadly he abandoned the search, but his remarkable
survey for ancient ships had been set in motion.

I thought of the exquisite bronze bust for three years, often specu-
lating on the use of a submarine for archaeology. A submarine
could penetrate such depths and remain for hours, moving rapidly
over the seabed and allowing us to cover vast areas we could not
otherwise investigate.

It remained only speculation until 1963. Then Mehmet Imbat,
nephew of the sponge dragger who had netted the veiled statue,
presented the Bodrum Museum with a new work of art: a tunic-clad
Negro youth, about one-third life size. He had found it not far from
Yassi Ada, dragging his sponge nets in three hundred feet of water.

We now had clues to two deep wrecks carrying Classical bronzes. I was determined to use a submarine. But how? The photograph of a two-man sport submarine on the New Products page of *Newsweek* magazine crystallized my thoughts. Perhaps we could afford our own.

Wlady Illing flew from Germany to help me shop for a submarine that fall. With a ninety-nine dollar "travel-anywhere" ticket he crisscrossed America by Greyhound bus—Chicago, San Francisco, New Orleans—appraising plans still on the drawing board, diving in untested contraptions, once helping first to build one. A midnight caller from a New Orleans hospital asked if I would be responsible for his hospital bills. A submarine accident? No, he had been mugged and robbed, his jaw broken across in two places. With jaws wired tightly shut he continued his search, living on milkshakes and peanut butter that he managed through a new gap in his front teeth.

Wlady and I had just decided which model we wanted to buy when I received a call from the Electric Boat Division of General Dynamics in Groton, Connecticut, largest builder of submarines in the world. Someone there had heard we were looking for a submarine. Could they build it for us? What they had in mind was far too expensive. Well, could they at least come to Philadelphia to talk?

Ted Coene, reminding me of my high-school science teacher in steel-rimmed glasses and crewcut hair; engineer Bob Toher, Boston-Irish sheriff of Groton; and Otto Mattner, a large man with a head for figures, entered my tiny office next day and looked for room to unroll their blueprints.

They quoted a price three times larger than I thought we could possibly raise. I said I was about to order a cheaper model that day. They pointed out the safety features they could build. I listened. What if we leave off this collar, I asked. How much would that reduce the price? Otto calculated, while Toher figured to see if we would lose any safety. The price dropped a bit. I examined the plans with care, liking most of what I saw, asking how much cost could be saved by eliminating this or that item.

I hurried between Dr. Rainey's office and my own; Toher and Coene made telephone calls to Groton. No research submarine had yet been built and privately sold in America. They were anxious to make the first.

The price continued to fall, but not far enough. I'm sorry, I finally admitted, we just can't afford it. Would I be willing to have dinner with them? I took them home first and located a bottle of gin that we poured over ice. The Electric Boat trio were good company. They took Ann and me to a Polynesian restaurant where we drank potent fruit punches from pineapples and coconut shells. Ann said she liked buying submarines. Still the price was too high. Coene said I drove a hard bargain. I said I wasn't used to high-pressure salesmanship. He laughed. As we parted he asked if I could meet them for breakfast. They called their wives, bought toothbrushes, and found a hotel room.

That night I talked to Don Rosencrantz, who was visiting us. Don, who knew the needs of underwater archaeology better than any engineer in the country, had just that week been offered a job with Electric Boat. I told him that if he decided to accept the job, I would do business with EB.

More figures, more discussion, more calculations over morning coffee. We finally reached a price for the basic sub with some features stripped off but plenty of gear left aboard. It was still more expensive than the model I had planned to order. Electric Boat agreed to absorb some of the cost of construction from its research and development funds. "I can find the rest of the money, I know I can," I said to Dr. Rainey in a rush of enthusiasm. He said to go ahead. We called the university purchasing department. It was just before Christmas. I needed the submarine in May.

After construction began in January, work continued around the clock. My car became a time machine, transporting me in a few hours from the thirteenth century B.C. in Philadelphia, where I was completing my doctoral dissertation on the Cape Gelidonya wreck, to the nuclear age of Groton. I became almost schizoid. Don said I should have become an engineer instead of an archaeologist. He defended me or his fellow engineers with impartiality in our differences over the submarine's design.

When the hull was almost completed, I scrambled up a ladder and lowered myself through the hatch. An entire telephone company seemed jammed into the five-foot sphere. Electrical wire and switches surrounded me. Panels presented a vast array of meters and controls: depth indicator, speed indicator, pressure gauges, gyroscopic compass, fathometer, communications systems, oxygen and carbon-dioxide meters, and speed and direction controls for the motors. The steel ball in which I sat was pierced with six viewing

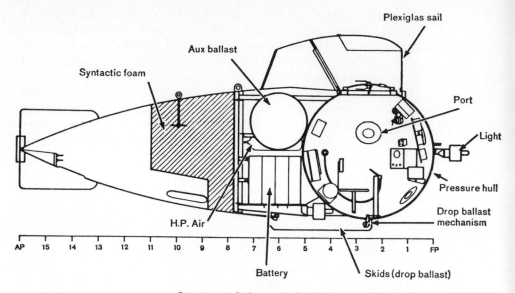

Section of the Asherah. *Syntactic foam, a solidified froth of air bubbles, buoys the stern of the submarine, which is heavily weighted with batteries.*

ports fitted with thick Plexiglas windows. Behind the round hull were ballast tanks, compressed-air tanks, and a ton of electric batteries, all protected and streamlined by a Fiberglas conical tail. A Plexiglas canopy protected the hatch so that it could be opened on the surface in minor waves.

The submarine was designed to descend safely to six hundred feet, with an air purifying system that would allow two men to breathe safely for twenty-four hours. Sixteen feet long, and weighing four and a half tons, the vessel would move at speeds up to four knots on its batteries, which were to be recharged every night.

The particular feature we needed for our work was the submarine's maneuverability. Electrically powered propellers on her sides could be rotated so that she could go forward, backward, up, or down, and could hover like a helicopter under water.

It was ironic that the relative poverty of our program had led us to such an expensive purchase. Never commanding the sums available to oceanographers and industry, we continually sought ways to lessen excavation costs. Our submarine would not be simply a mobile observation capsule for underwater search. I was convinced it could be a work vehicle, cutting time and therefore cost from excavations as well. I outlined for Don and Julian Whittlesey the concept for a stereophotography system that would allow us to "fly" over wrecks, mapping them quickly with aerial survey techniques; they said they could work out the details. The submarine was also so maneuverable that a simple arm, made of coat hangers if necessary, could hold a portable air lift, allowing two men to excavate more in a day than was possible with a large team of divers. A slightly more complex manipulator could place artifacts into a basket and fill a lifting balloon to send them to the surface. The vessel could also be used as a control center from which an excavation director could watch teams of divers working in rotation, directing them by underwater loudspeaker.

I presented some of these ideas later at the Woods Hole Oceanographic Institute, at a symposium on the use of manned research submersibles. Al Vine, designer of Woods Hole's famed *Alvin,* launched soon after our submarine, pointed to a high-ranking officer: "I wish you could have heard what he said after your talk. He said the navy ought to rethink its entire concept of using research submarines."

The day of the launching, Ann was given a wooden replica of a champagne bottle to practice her swing before the ceremony. She walked the length of the graving dock, studying intently a mammoth nuclear submarine tied alongside for repairs. She passed our tiny craft, almost invisible under blue bunting in the middle of the pier, and reached the end.

"Where's *your* submarine, George?" she asked in bewilderment.

When we stepped from a limousine for the actual christening later in the day, I saw familiar faces in the crowd: Rodney Young and others from the University Museum, including James Pritchard, curator of Biblical Archaeology, who had suggested we name our new submarine after Asherah, Phoenician goddess of the sea; Dr. Melvin Payne led a contingent from the National Geographic Society, which, with the National Science Foundation, had donated a large part of the submarine's cost. Most of the old Yassi Ada crew were there, their personal lives somehow inextricably meshed with underwater archaeology: Don Rosencrantz introduced Eric Ryan to Joyce, Eric's future wife, at a celebration dinner; David and Susan Owen came directly from their wedding in Boston so David could be on hand for scheduled sea trials.

Ann, carrying a bouquet of red, white, and blue carnations, was escorted by Dr. Herman Sheets, Chief Research and Development Engineer of Electric Boat, as flashbulbs popped and newsreel cameras for the television networks ground. Following the invocation, Dr. Sheets spoke of the importance of the first nonmilitary submarine launched by the Electric Boat Company in its sixty-year history. He read a congratulatory telegram to us from the crew of the *Trieste,* the bathyscaphe, which had gone to the deepest part of the oceans, more than six miles down. I said a few words on the purpose of our submersible, and Admiral A.I. McKee, once the navy's chief submarine designer, unzipped its covering of bunting.

Ann smashed the champagne bottle: "I christen thee *Asherah.*"

The flags of the University of Pennsylvania and the National Geographic Society fluttered next to the Stars and Stripes as loudspeakers blared "Anchors Aweigh" from above. A large gantry crane lifted the *Asherah* into the air ("Isn't it cute!" a woman's voice exclaimed), and lowered her gently into the Thames River as the coast guard band and chorus, to the surprise of a squadron of saluting naval officers, changed to "Hail Pennsylvania."

Leaving Ann, who remained to ship the submarine, I set sail almost immediately for Turkey. In mid-Atlantic I was paged to come to the *Olympia*'s radio office.

"George! The freighter leaves tomorrow . . ." I barely recognized Ann's voice. "The American State Department won't let the *Asherah* go . . . *static* . . . needs official . . . *garble* . . . number . . . call back . . ."

I ransacked my luggage for something that seemed official. Did the State Department think anyone was dumb enough to have a submarine built and shipped to Turkey without having permission to use it there? We had even arranged to train Yüksel Eğdemir as *Asherah*'s pilot so that a Turkish archaeologist would be always at her controls during working dives. I could find nothing except my Yassi Ada excavation permit.

I returned Ann's call, but our words were fragmented by electrical interference. She could understand nothing I said.

We had, a year earlier, met Ambassador Menemengioglu of Turkey, after showing a film on our work at the National Geographic Society. He had inquired politely if there was anything he could do for us; we said no, everything was going smoothly. Ann and Dr. Rainey now called on him for help. After they had explained the

The sponge boat Mandalinçi *is moored directly over the Bronze Age wreck during its excavation in 1960. The ancient vessel sank between rocky islands strung out from Cape Gelidonya, rising in the distance.*

*Grid wires enable Susan Womer to make scale draw-
ings of the Byzantine cargo (above). The pottery of a
Roman wreck has already been removed (below), as
Fred van Doorninck cleans its hull for mapping.*

Using a plane table similar to those used by surveyors on land, Claude Duthuit sights through an alidade to take a fix on a surveyors' pole held by another diver on the Byzantine wreck.

"You've built a city down there!" exclaimed a veteran diver the first time he saw the technology we had assembled on a Roman wreck 140 feet deep. Although no more than four divers normally worked together, artist Davis Meltzer has here combined all of their activities into a single scene. The submarine *Asherah* glides over the site, stroboscopic flashes lighting the cargo below for stereophotography. A television camera in the center of the camera bracket gives the *Asherah*'s crew a view of what they photograph. The scaffolding of angle iron constructed over the wreck provides support for a supplemental photo tower and also divides the wreck into convenient compartments for controlled excavation. On the lower edge of the site, a diver moves an aluminum air-lift pipe along 70 feet of track, sucking up sand forced down the slope from the wreck by a high-pressure water jet. Another diver guides an electronic metal detector near the underwater telephone booth, an air-filled Plexiglas dome anchored to heavy steel plates. Amphoras rise to the surface in a basket suspended below a lifting balloon, just filled with air, as more delicate wood fragments are carried to nearby Yassi Ada in a wire basket held by four divers. In the distance, a spherical underwater decompression chamber enables excavators to make longer dives by allowing them to decompress for long periods inside in dry comfort.

Chief diver Bob Henry takes photographs from predetermined marks on a horizontal bar floating over the Roman wreck at Yassi Ada. Every two pictures forms a stereo pair for mapping. (above)

Stereo pairs, taken above, are projected in red and green light through a Multiplex, enabling Jeremy Green, wearing similarly colored lenses, to see and draw the wreck in three dimensions.

Only about 10 percent of the Byzantine ship's hull shown in red remained below its cargo of nearly a thousand globular wine jars, but careful study of these fragments (shown in red) over many years has allowed the accurate reconstruction of the ship (shown in blue) depicted in Chapter 9.

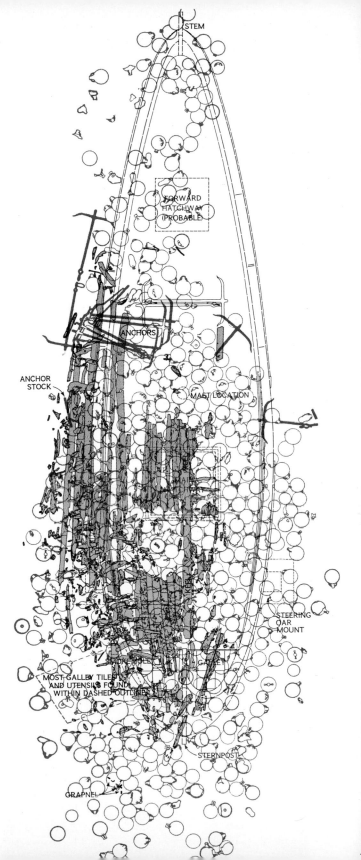

STEM

FORWARD
HATCHWAY
(PROBABLE)

ANCHORS

ANCHOR
STOCK

MAST LOCATION

KEEL

STEERING
OAR
MOUNT

MOST GALLEY TILES
AND UTENSILS FOUND
WITHIN DASHED OUTLINE

STERNPOST

GRAPNEL

PREPARED FROM DRAWINGS BY
FREDERICK H. VAN DOORNINCK, JR.,
BY THE GEOGRAPHIC ART DIVISION,
© NATIONAL GEOGRAPHIC SOCIETY.

The fourth-century Roman ship produced the usual assortment of well-preserved cooking and table wares found on ancient wrecks. The author, Ann Bass, and Yüksel Eğdemir inspect the finds on Yassi Ada.

situation, he assured the American State Department that all was in order. The *Asherah* was loaded that day.

At the same time, a heavier cargo was destined for the Mediterranean. To aid our work, the United States Navy had lent us a sixty-five-foot support vessel, the *Virazon.* Captain Edward Snyder, later oceanographer of the navy, explained their willingness to help: "You can test underwater equipment so much more cheaply than we can."

It was an understatement. Philadelphia yachtsman Lloyd Wells volunteered to skipper the *Virazon,* commanding a volunteer crew including first-rate engineer Gerald Stern. The Lykes Brothers Steamship Company ferried the sixty-five-ton vessel as deck cargo from her berth in Galveston as far as Greece, without charge. Don Rosencrantz and Julian Whittlesey designed our new submarine mapping equipment on their own time, and then Don obtained a leave of absence from Electric Boat to be in charge of the *Asherah* in Turkey. I paid not a cent in salary for the *Asherah*'s operation during the entire project.

As the museum's fleet rendezvoused in the Mediterranean, we completed the excavation of the Byzantine wreck at Yassi Ada, bringing up the last pieces, carrying fragments of wood and iron to

The sixty-five ton Virazon *is lifted from Galveston harbor for her voyage to the Aegean as deck cargo on the* Ruth Lykes.

land. Michael Katzev, a meticulous new archaeology student on the team, took charge of our iron concretions, casting over a hundred tools. Specializing in art history, he was so intrigued by the probability of finding more Classical sculpture beneath the sea that he transferred from Columbia University to the University of Pennsylvania to work more closely with us. He and Susan Womer met on the island; within two years they were married.

A message from our customs broker brought me to Izmir for the arrival of the *Asherah.* I saw a large truck parked by the side of the road and leaned against it, waiting for its driver to return.

"How many tons can you carry?"

"Six."

"If you drive very slowly, can you carry more?"

"Evet, efendim." Yes, sir.

We arrived at the docks shortly after sunup, and an eight-ton crate was lowered from a ship onto the truck. Customs went quickly. The driver crept slowly over the often bumpy road to Güllük, the harbor nearest Yassi Ada with a crane large enough to unload the submarine. The crane was there only temporarily, for installation of a new quay; we hoped it would still be there at sum-

Rubber casts made in the natural molds of concretion that formed over iron tools preserve the finest details of the original objects.

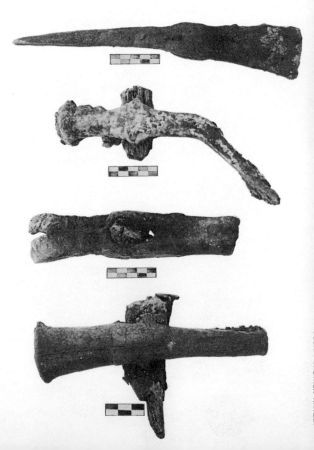

mer's end to lift the sub out of the sea again. I processed ten crates of support equipment through customs, and set out after the truck.

A Bodrum fishing boat towed the *Asherah,* a great orange ice-cream cone floating on its side, to Yassi Ada where she was anchored like a rowboat in shallow water for the rest of the summer of 1964.

There had been no time to complete sea trials in Groton. Electric Boat sent engineer Bill Beran to continue work with Don in Turkey. Bill took me for my first dive. We were rowed to the submarine and stepped barefoot over the Plexiglas conning tower onto the polished steel hatch seating. I lowered myself with both hands, stepping first onto my seat and then onto the damp, curving floor. It was cold inside, the air thick with the unmistakable smell of electric wiring and metal.

Bill ran over a check list printed on an aluminum board. Then, standing on his seat, head and shoulders rising through the hatch into our transparent conning tower, he motioned Larry to cast us off. Larry unhooked two shackles and snorkeled clear of the propellers as Bill threw both motors of the *Asherah* into reverse, backing us into open water. Bill then dropped down beside me, pulling the hatch cover after him with a reverberating clang and dogging it in

Drawings of the original tools as they looked at the time of the wreck, before concretions formed.

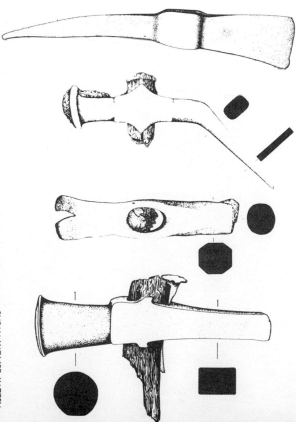

place. I could see nothing but blue water through the bottom port between my feet. A twist of a knob sent air bubbling up and out of our main flotation tank. Soon blue water covered the upper ports as well. We were now heavy, but not completely submerged. A last bubble of air was trapped under the Fiberglas body which surrounded the batteries and air tanks; the tail was meant to be flooded, the batteries encased in a protective block of something like solidified strawberry jam. Bill turned both propellers straight up and eased the speed control levers forward. The whirr of the motors rose to a high whine which, when it reached the level of a turbine scream, turned suddenly into a vast rumble, almost an audible sign of strain as he forced the last air from the fairing. We had burst through the surface barrier and had become an underwater creature, our buoyancy gone. Bill throttled back on the engines and, watching the gyrocompass, guided us toward the wreck, now giving more power to the starboard motor, now to the port. As we followed the steep slope our tail bumped several times, hard.

With motors slightly depressed, the Asherah *rises from the seabed near Yassi Ada. The empty bracket is for mounting stereo cameras when needed.*

We settled on a flat, sandy bottom where he could trim ballast to neutral buoyancy; from this time all movement came from the direction of the propellers. Only in emergency might he need to blow the ballast tanks to send us hurtling upward out of control; if that should fail, a turn of the red handle at my feet would drop half a ton of metal. I looked out at the seaweed and fish.

"What do you think of her?" he asked.

"Great." I studied one of the still confusing number of gauges above and before me. It read 50. "When will you take her on down?"

"We're at two hundred feet. It doesn't get any deeper around here," Bill said. He added politely, as he pointed to another dial, "This is the depth gauge over here."

It was little different from the 120 feet in which we dived daily; the light level seemed about the same. We droned westward, back up toward the wreck, and set down just beside it. I watched Lloyd Wells and Wlady test a water jet from the *Virazon*'s pumps. We talked to the divers over a loudspeaker. They could hear us, but not well.

Every few minutes Bill touched the speed control of one of the twin motors and we pivoted slightly on the seabed to get a different view of the wreck. I was impressed by the ease with which we could inch over the bottom, as delicately as a diver.

"Let's have a look at the reef before we go up," I suggested.

We followed a trail of broken pottery up the slope until the flicker of sunlight scattered by waves breaking over the reef indicated we were near the surface.

"We're too close," I thought. "Why doesn't he turn?"

Bill struggled with the controls. He threw the motors into full reverse as the surge of a breaker caught us, still submerged, and pressed us on toward the menacing rocks. The motors weren't powerful enough. An obelisk of stone loomed before my bottom port, aimed straight at me. I ducked back instinctively as the center of the window struck. We ground to a sickening halt and then twisted sideways as the momentum of a ton of batteries carried the tail onward toward the reef. We bumped heavily along the rocky ledge. The Plexiglas window, thick as those that had gone with the bathyscaphe to the bottom of the ocean, cracked under the impact. Water seeped in. Without thinking, I grasped the knob that would open a pipe to our air supply, to fill the sphere with high-pressure air to keep us from filling with water and tumbling back down the slope into the depths below. It wasn't necessary. The window held. We sweated profusely, dressed only in bathing suits, as water rose over our feet. And then we laughed.

We replaced the broken window after hauling the *Asherah* as far out of water as possible, ten of us, knee deep, playing tug-of-war with a submarine.

Don and Yüksel operated the *Asherah* after Bill Beran returned to America. Yüksel, with the reflexes and coordination that had made him an international fencer, became a superb pilot. Don took turns at the controls, but more often ran the new mapping system. He had mounted two aerial survey cameras in waterproof housings about six feet apart on a bar bolted to the submarine's nose. When he pressed a button inside, the pair of cameras took pictures simultaneously with the flash of two strobe lights and then recocked their shutters and advanced their own film automatically, ready for another stereo pair. We ran tests on artificial targets set only 50 feet deep before proceeding to map the Late Roman wreck, 140 feet deep, on which our barge anchors had caught during the storm that ended the 1961 season. We had decided that it would be the next site we would excavate.

Hundreds of miles to the east, hostilities between the Greek and Turkish populations of Cyprus threatened to bring Greece and Turkey, themselves, into direct conflict over that newly independent island nation. We followed the mounting troubles by radio. Turkish jets bombed Cyprus, followed by rumors of an imminent Turkish invasion.

Yassi Ada lies almost exactly on the invisible border that divides Turkish and Greek waters. Our neat rows of identical tents and our navy ship anchored just off shore gave the appearance of a military base. Messages radioed from Yassi Ada to the *Asherah* may have sounded ominous to military intelligence. We feared that neither side might remember who we were if war broke out. Eric painted a huge American flag on the roof of *Virazon*'s cabin, and we worked a few more days. Then we had had enough. Jets screamed low overhead. In one day we broke camp completely, loading everything onto the barge before nightfall.

We headed for Bodrum in total darkness, the *Virazon* towing the barge which in turn towed the *Asherah*. Strung out over more than a hundred yards, the barge and submarine lit with kerosene lanterns, flashlights, and whatever else we could find, we must have resembled some strange, huge ship slipping through the channel between Turkey and the nearby Greek islands. Without warning a floodlight blinded us, flashing a signal from only yards away.

"What does it say, George? You were a signal officer."

I searched my memory in vain for the code letters for *friend,* but it didn't matter—I didn't know what language to send it in.

"Maybe they're saying to identify ourselves or be blown out of the water."

We proceeded slowly, our new and silent partner invisible somewhere in the inky darkness. Next day the commander of Bodrum's coastal patrol boat hailed Yüksel:

"Why didn't you answer us last night? We asked if you needed any help."

Leaving David Owen in charge of the expedition, I returned to the University of Pennsylvania to begin my first year of teaching. A few days later David had the submarine towed back to Yassi Ada. During one dive, the *Asherah* was "flown" in two passes over the Roman wreck. Don took a series of overlapping pairs of photographs on each pass, completely covering the site. Before an accurate plan with elevation measurements could be made from these pictures, fifty-six hours of laboratory work with the instruments of Holland's International Training Center for Aerial Survey were needed. But the underwater work had taken less than half an hour. It would have taken a dozen archaeologists with aqualungs, using the best mapping methods previously devised, many weeks of diving to do the same job. Within a few years, most research submarines built would use our system.

There had been no time for the *Asherah* to search for deep wrecks that summer. Before we used her again, in 1967, she stayed busy for three years as we rented her out for a variety of missions. For the United States Bureau of Commercial Fisheries and the University of Hawaii, she was used to study fish in the Pacific, locating deep and unknown lobster beds off Hawaii. She carried equipment to video-tape six miles of electronic cable 180 feet under the Rosario Straits in Washington state for the Interior Department, and went to Nova Scotia and Rhode Island for marine biology. The United States Navy flew her to the Caribbean where she successfully located a lost object of unidentified nature near Puerto Rico.

CHAPTER VIII
Putting It Together

$\sim\sim\sim\sim\sim\sim\sim\sim\sim\sim\sim\sim\sim\sim\sim\sim\sim$
$\sim\sim\sim\sim\sim\sim\sim\sim\sim\sim\sim\sim\sim\sim\sim\sim\sim$
$\sim\sim\sim\sim\sim\sim\sim\sim\sim\sim\sim\sim\sim\sim\sim\sim\sim$

THE quantity of material excavated in the Byzantine ship was so large and varied that, to speed its publication, I farmed out separate categories of artifacts to other scholars, asking each to write a chapter for the final report, much as I had for the book on the Cape Gelidonya wreck.

I was concerned mainly with the pottery, both galley wares and cargo. In addition, I wrote a section on the techniques of the excavation, to follow an introduction by Peter Throckmorton on the discovery of the wreck. I planned to tie it all together in a concluding chapter.

It was to Fred van Doorninck that fully half the publication would fall. I knew, during the course of excavation, that we would learn some details of Byzantine ship construction from the bits and pieces of wood we so carefully mapped and raised. But when I saw the fragmentary state of the entire, uncovered hull, I thought most of it had little more value than kindling. Other marine archaeologists had published, and continue to publish, "reconstructions" of Roman ships based mostly on contemporaneous representations of ships on mosaics, reliefs, and wall paintings, with details added here and there from their excavations. Fred thought that in our case much more was possible, and asked if he could make the attempt.

For the next three years he worked. Seldom in that time did I call or visit his home in Princeton that he was not hunched over a drawing board, matching the angles and sizes of nail and bolt holes, pulling together isolated bits of information from his detailed notes and plans. He was determined to learn the lines of an ancient seagoing ship from the slim evidence of its wreckage, something never before tried on an underwater excavation.

His approach was usually ingenious, sometimes clairvoyant.

He measured the cavities left by corroded iron anchors in our largest uncast concretions with such accuracy that he later could calculate the volume of metal originally in each anchor. He multiplied the results by the specific gravity of iron with a high carbon content, the kind used in Roman times, to determine the original weights of the anchors and their iron stocks. Some intuition then led him to observe that two stocks weighed close to 50 and 100 Roman pounds of 315 grams to the pound, and that most of the anchors weighed either 250 or 450 Roman pounds. This suggested to him that medieval statutes, specifying the number and weights of anchors merchant ships of different sizes were required to carry, had their origins in the Byzantine period.

Terracotta tiles had been raised from most Roman shipwrecks previously examined by divers, but their purpose on even partially excavated ships was debated: were they cargo, roofing, or material from cooking facilities? Fred fitted and matched our fragments until he knew exactly where each pantile and cover tile had lain on the galley roof; square hearth tiles from the cook's firebox had been supported by iron bars revealed to him only by their modern rubber casts.

He slowly drew a picture of the ship from barely visible clues. By tracing every score line, and following the angle of every cutting, and studying the position of every artifact on his plans, he learned the level of the deck, and the locations of the main cargo hatch, the mast, the steering sweeps, and the bulkhead separating cargo from galley, although not a trace of any of these had been preserved.

Fred's most important discovery was that the ship provided the first evidence for the beginning of modern shipbuilding techniques.

Today, in making a wooden hull, a boat builder usually constructs a skeleton of keel, stem, sternpost, and ribs over which he nails a skin of planking. The Greek or Roman shipwright, however, built his hull up with planks directly from the keel, without ribs, holding the planks together and in place with hundreds or thousands of mortise-and-tenon joints in the plank edges; ribs were added later, sometimes almost as an afterthought.

The seventh-century wreck at Yassi Ada had been built in the old "shell-first" manner up to the waterline; but then, probably to save labor and money, the shipwright simply added ribs and nailed the rest of the planks over them in the modern manner.

Fred's results were presented in his 1967 doctoral dissertation, "The Seventh-Century Byzantine Ship at Yassi Ada. Some Contributions to the History of Naval Architecture." They were more original and more carefully thought out than many reconstructions I had seen of land architectural remains.

Fred came back from his first job interview shaken.

"George, I really thought you were paranoid. I just didn't believe you. Everything went well until they asked me what I wrote my doctoral dissertation on, and when I said it was on a Byzantine shipwreck they broke into laughter. What's funny about it?"

David Owen received his Ph.D. two years later in Ancient Near Eastern languages, specializing in cuneiform economic texts, a subject on which he has published broadly. After his first interview, I later learned, one of the faculty members on the interviewing committee blurted out: "We want an historian, not a *skin diver!*"

It was sometimes hard, in those days, to convince other serious students that they could continue diving without jeopardizing their careers. One of the best, from England, said that his professor didn't think much of underwater archaeology, so he had better not join us again. Michael Katzev, about that time, swore he would never write a dissertation on a nautical subject; he didn't want to be branded an "underwater archaeologist."

Their fears were not exaggerated. Now my students were learning, as only they could at first hand, what I had told them: our work was scorned by perhaps a majority of Classical archaeologists. This was something my colleagues in the museum never believed nor understood, but it often made life miserable.

I encountered this attitude as early as 1961, when one of America's most influential archaeologists commented on "this silly business you do under water."

Silly? I was perplexed and bewildered. We had just excavated the largest and best-dated hoard of seventh-century pottery ever found, something that could help him immensely in his present research, yet he called our work silly. He said underwater archaeology was unscientific and destructive, and compared us to the amateur divers who pulled occasional broken amphoras from the Aegean.

I had thought that my published excavation reports made clear the exact nature and purpose of our work. Now I began my first book, *Archaeology Under Water,* as a long essay to explain more precisely what we did. It opened with the suggestion that archaeology under water should not be called "underwater archaeology" but simply "archaeology":

> We do not speak of those working on the top of Nimrud Dagh in Turkey as mountain archaeologists, nor those at Tikal in Guatemala as jungle archaeologists. They are all people who are trying to answer questions regarding man's past, and they are adaptable in being able to excavate and interpret ancient buildings, tombs, and even entire cities with the artifacts which they contain. Is the study of an ancient ship and its cargo, or the survey of toppled harbor walls somehow different? That such remains may lie under water entails the use of different tools and techniques in their study, just as the survey of a large area on land, using aerial photographs, magnetic detectors, and drills, requires a procedure other than excavating the stone artifacts and bones in a Palaeolithic cave. The basic aim in all these cases is the same. It is all archaeology.

The message was lost. My next book, *Cape Gelidonya,* the study of a Bronze Age site, was given by a major archaeological journal to a reviewer chosen for expertise in diving rather than Bronze Age archaeology. I was further disappointed when a Turkish official questioned my application to excavate a Bronze Age site on land because, as he wrote, I was an "underwater archaeologist." I grew weary of being asked by colleagues when I planned to get back to "real archaeology."

Still, I was luckier than the younger members of my excavation staffs. My ability to gain a livelihood was not threatened. Froelich Rainey, director of the University Museum, and Rodney Young, chairman of my department, continued to see the promise of this new field.

Gradually old prejudices have faded. But the youthful innocence and exuberance of our first two years in underwater archaeology had been crushed. Never again would we attract in such a short time so many who would remain in our discipline.

Because of this attitude prevailing among humanists, most of our excavation funds had come from sources more concerned with underwater technology than with historical results. Some potential sponsors, unfamiliar with archaeology, were aghast to learn that laws prohibit antiquities from leaving almost all Mediterranean countries:

"You get nothing? You mean you're doing all this for Turkish museums? You spend the money and do the work, and they get the objects? You're being exploited!"

It is hard to correct this old-fashioned concept of archaeology as simply the collecting of antiquities, to explain that the modern archaeologist is interested in the knowledge resulting from his excavation, and that—with notes, photographs, plans, and drawings— he doesn't need the actual finds.

"Astronomers can photograph the stars, map them, and measure them," I have pointed out, "but they can't own them. This doesn't stop support for observatories."

Is it not preferable to keep the remains of a wreck together in one Turkish museum, where they can be viewed as a unit, than to divide them between two continents? In our day of mass communication and international travel, the rationale for hauling antiquities back to Europe and America in the nineteenth and early twentieth centuries, when the only window to the past was the glass of a dusty museum case, is obsolete.

One of the reasons there is so little understanding of scientific archaeology is that archaeologists, themselves, have rarely published outside their relatively obscure journals. There is a tradition in Classical archaeology that it is better not to publish at all than to write for the public.

Because there is misunderstanding about archaeology in general, continuing debate over the respective roles of archaeologists and divers in marine archaeology is largely meaningless.

During a panel discussion at a diving conference, I was berated for saying that underwater excavations should be left to trained archaeologists. The two intelligent, skilled divers who faced me—lawyers by profession—rightly pointed out that they could do any one of the things I had just explained in an illustrated talk on excavation techniques.

I tried to make clear that my lecture had been really more about *diving* than archaeology, that recording and excavating a site were only first steps. Most divers can excavate well, and amateur divers fill many of the positions requiring photographic, artistic, or mechanical skills on my expeditions. Further, amateur divers have played the major role in underwater surveys, most sites under water, as on land, having been found by nonspecialists.

The archaeologist, however, must be ultimately responsible for the collection and recording of the data he must interpret and publish. The academic degrees he usually has obtained are merely symbols that he is familiar with ancient history and languages, and that he has learned to organize, interpret, and present archaeological material in a satisfactory manner. He does not claim they make him more intelligent.

The debate continues. Any diver who systemmatically salvages artifacts from ancient ships is referred to in the press as an archaeologist, which is the same as saying that the farmer who carefully digs the Indian mound in his corn field is an archaeologist. This is one more indication that underwater archaeology is not yet accepted, even in the public mind, as "real archaeology."

During these often frustrating middle years, good things also came our way. One of these good things was J. Richard Steffy.

Dick Steffy became part of our group simply because he was the first of dozens of model builders to approach me. He had read about the Byzantine wreck in the *National Geographic,* and wrote to ask if he might try to build a model of it. I saw no reason why not. We met soon after.

His hands were strong and hard, his face more weather-lined than ours, and he was a bit older than any of us, somewhere in his forties. He ran a business of installing and maintaining factory electrical systems, but had grown up spending spare moments in boat yards and maritime museums, and had served in the navy. He wasn't interested in a display model, he said. He wanted to know what could be learned of the ship through building models.

He and Fred began a running correspondence, and Dick soon had a scale drawing of every timber fragment from the ship, many at full size. His dining room table became a permanent bed for the six-foot models he built.

I had always been glad that Fred was no professional sailor, that he knew little about ship construction, that he had no preconceived ideas about the structure of the ship before he began his work. I still feel that way. He would have assumed too much, drawn conclusions too easily, as I had seen others do, instead of letting the evidence take him wherever it led. At this point, however, Dick's knowledge

The reconstructed stern of the Byzantine ship, show-ing the interior of the galley with its firebox for cook-ing.

STORAGE

STORAGE

FRED VAN DOORNINCK, J.R. STEFFY, & SUSAN WOMER KATZEV

of ships and how they worked was an invaluable aid to new discoveries.

While Dick was building and destroying his first twelve "working" models, learning something new from each, I spent a sabbatical year in England to complete my own end of the research. Travels to European museums took me to Rumania, where some of the best parallels for our pottery were found.

It was there, on the coast of the Black Sea at Tomis (modern Constanza), that I walked through a port used and destroyed by earthquake less than a century before our ship sank. Inside the great vaulted storerooms and shops, which stretched a hundred yards along the ancient harbor front, I saw amphoras almost identical to all the types from Yassi Ada, holding pigments, resin, and iron nails. Stacks of iron anchors like those Fred studied so carefully, lamps like those from our lost ship, and weights for measuring supplies were also there. It was obviously a ship's chandlery. As I looked out across the dry land fill, which was once a bay, I pictured our captain outfitting his ship from such shops. I was overwhelmed at that moment, as never before or since, by a vivid sense of reality for our doomed argosy.

Soon after, on my return to England, I received drafts of most chapters for the final publication of the Byzantine ship. Joan Fagerlie, of the American Numismatic Society, had studied the seventy coins of gold and copper. Other assemblages of artifacts had been studied by former students in my seminars at the University of Pennsylvania, most now teaching archaeology elsewhere: the twenty-four lamps by Karen Vitelli, of the University of Maryland; balance-pan weights and steelyards by Kenneth Sams, at the University of North Carolina; more than a hundred corroded iron tools reconstructed in rubber, by Michael Katzev at Oberlin College; the miscellaneous finds of bronze, copper, glass, stone and wood, by Susan Womer Katzev; and the lead fishing weights by Peter Kuniholm, whose detailed examination of ancient and modern fishing techniques explained our astonishing variety of lead sinkers used for different types of fish at different times of the year.

Fred and Dick are still at work on their final restoration of the ship, but by 1970 we could at last begin to tell the story of its last voyage. By then we had also excavated a fourth-century A.D. wreck with which to compare it.

CHAPTER IX

A.D. 625

~~~~~~
~~~~~~
~~~~~~

THE merchant ordered his ship built small. Of only sixty tons' burden, she would be tiny compared to the great freighters found in state merchant fleets of the past. Like many of the independent ship owners, whose numbers increased in the seventh-century Byzantine Empire, he could not afford a larger vessel. The days were over when ships of twice its burden were considered small, and imperial Roman grain carriers plying between Alexandria and Rome carried more than 1,200 tons.

A cypress keel was laid in a shipyard probably located in the Aegean, in the Black Sea, or in the waters between. On the keel, which was about forty feet long, was mounted a high, curved sternpost of the same wood; the ship's stem was probably also made of cypress. Once the spine of the hull had been completed the shipwrights went on to construct the sides.

They did not, as we would do today, first build a complete skeleton by adding ribs to the spine and then cover the frame with planking. Neither did they follow the practice, customary in earlier centuries, of first building the hull by fastening its planks edge to edge with a series of mortise-and-tenon joints no more than four inches apart along the full length of each strake, or strip of plank-

ing, and then adding the ribs. Seventh-century construction fell somewhere between these two methods; it represents the continuation of a trend, starting two or three centuries earlier, that cut down the investment in labor required to build hulls in the earlier Greco-Roman style, perhaps another reflection of the modest amounts private entrepreneurs could invest in shipping.

Selecting pine planks, the shipwrights cut mortices in them every three feet or so and fastened the planks together edge to edge by inserting loosely fitted tenons made of oak. The hull was built up from the keel in this fashion, one strake at a time, for several rows of planking. Then elm floors, or short "ribs," were placed inside and secured in place with iron nails driven through the pine strakes from outside. Another four or five strakes were added to bring the hull shell to the turn of the bilge, and longer floors were inserted. The shell was then completed to the waterline and the remainder of the "ribbing," half-frames, and futtocks, added. Internal hull planking (ceiling) was installed next. Finally, the heavy-timbered hull sides were completed by bolting four pairs of heavier strakes, or wales, to the ribs and filling the spaces between them by nailing additional planks to the ribs without mortise-and-tenon joining.

This kind of compromise with earlier Greco-Roman practice had been on the rise for at least 250 years. The hull of a ship built in the fourth century, about 225 years earlier, was made with carefully mortised planking; the mortising continued at least up to the deck level and possibly all the way to the gunwale. The planks were fixed to the ribs with treenails—long wooden dowels —rather than iron nails, and smaller dowels held each tenon securely in place. Even by then, however, the mortise-and-tenon joints were spaced about seven inches apart, or considerably farther apart than before. The trend was destined to continue. The practice of fastening the planks to the ribs with iron nails and omitting mortise-and-tenon joints, found only above the waterline in the seventh-century ship, advanced until the strength of a hull came to depend exclusively on the bonds between the ribs and the planking, as is true today, and mortise-and-tenon hull-stiffening disappeared.

Deck beams ran across the width of the merchant's hull, supported at their ends by short L-shaped timbers. The ship was completely decked except for the galley area at the stern and a hatch aft of the single, centrally located mast; there may also have been a smaller hatch forward. Deck beams projected beyond the hull on each side to form a pair of rectangular structures where the steering oars were mounted.

The finished ship was just under seventy feet long, with a streamlined hull and a beam of only seventeen feet. This is a length-to-width ratio of four to one, which is quite slender for a cargo vessel. The fourth-century vessel mentioned above had been beamier; its ratio was roughly two and one-half to one. Swifter merchant vessels were needed in the seventh century, it is believed, to outrun the increased number of hostile ships on the sea.

When the slim merchantman was ready for launching, its owner visited a ship chandler to outfit the vessel. Stacked against a wall, perhaps in a large vaulted chamber like those at Tomis, were iron anchors with removable stocks. The owner bought at least eleven from the chandler, and also obtained a clawlike grapnel, probably for the ship's boat.

Why were there so many anchors? Due to their extreme lightness, the captain must have occasionally found it necessary to use four bower anchors, carried ready for use in the forward quarter of the ship, simultaneously. The shanks and arms of the anchors were quite thin and the flukes poorly developed, so such anchors were undoubtedly often broken. Consequently, the captain carried four spare bowers piled on the deck nearby. At the bottom of the pile lay three heavier sheet anchors to be used as a last resort. The uniformity of the weights of the anchors suggests statutes requiring vessels of various classes to carry a minimum number of anchors of specified sizes, as in later times.

The chandlery patronized by the owner offered a variety of resins for sale. His ship had already been coated with resin below the waterline, inside and out. Now he obtained a smaller amount to be melted on board in a cheap cooking pot and applied as needed to seal the pores of clay pitchers and other containers for wine. The chandlery also offered pigments for paint and jars full of iron nails. We do not know whether or not the owner painted his ship, although ships of earlier and later times were often described as brightly colored. He did buy several bags of nails, probably with shipboard repairs in mind.

Literary accounts of the period mention skins for covering deck cargo in foul weather, as well as sails and hemp rope, and all of these the owner may have got at the chandlery. We are certain that

RICHARD SCHLECHT

he bought twenty-four oil lamps, perhaps made from molds known to have been kept on hand in at least the chandlery at Tomis.

With the new ship almost ready for sea it was time to assemble a crew. We need not depend entirely on our imagination in reconstructing the roster; a document of the seventh century or slightly later, known as the Rhodian sea law, lists a regular ship's company of the day and assigns to each member his proper share in the profits of a successful venture. First is the naukleros, the shipowner or the captain or both, who receives two shares. Next are the kybernetes, the helmsman; the proreus, the "prow officer"; the naupagos, the ship's carpenter; and the karabites, the boatswain. Each receives a share and a half. This completes the list of officers; the nautai, or seamen, who follow on the roster receive a single share each. Last is the lowliest member of the crew, the parascharites. The approximate meaning of the word is "gut-slitter," and in this context it may mean cook. At any rate, his stake in the voyage is only half a share.

The captain of the vessel was named Georgios. He was probably also the ship owner, or perhaps a part owner. The finest scale on the ship, a bronze balance of the kind called a steelyard, had his name

punched in it in Greek letters to read Georgiou Presbyterou Nauk-
lerou. *That is to say that the steelyard beam belonged to "Georgios
Elder (or Senior), Owner/Sea Captain." The inscription presents
problems in spite of its simplicity. Christianity was a strong ele-
ment in every aspect of Byzantine life; was Captain Georgios a*
presbyteros, *an elder of the church? Or does the word have some
other meaning here?*

*Several passages in the Rhodian sea law indicate that sometimes
there was more than one captain aboard a vessel. How would one
have distinguished between two captains? Should Georgios' title
perhaps be read as "Georgios, Senior Sea Captain"? In the previous
century the name of one* Nicholas Naukleros Mesatos *had been
inscribed on a baptismal basin in a church in southwest Asia Minor.* Mesatos *is derived from* mesos, *meaning middle, and it has
been suggested that Nicholas might have been something such as
a "middling sea captain," that is an officer junior to a senior sea
captain. No one accepts this completely. In its support, however, it
should be noted that* mesonautai *are mentioned in the literature
of the sixth century and it is believed that the term applied to a
junior grade of* nautai *or regular seamen.*

*The next officer listed in the sea law, the helmsman, possibly
stood on a high wooden platform just forward of the galley, in
order to man the giant steering oars. The known placement of the
steering oars suggests the presence of such a platform, similar to
those known from earlier Roman ship representations.*

*A prow officer, if one was on board, may have had charge of the
anchors, as well as the conical sounding lead with a hollow for the
tallow or wax that picked up samples of the bottom.*

*The ship's carpenter stored his tool chest in a locker in the gal-
ley's forward wall. In it were iron tools, including an axe, adzes, a
hammer-adze, a claw hammer, hammers for metalworking, chisels,
gouges, punches, files, drill bits, dividers, an awl, assorted knives,
and numerous nails and tacks. A folded sheet of lead and some
waste from lead casting suggest that various fittings, as well as
additional fishing weights, were made on board the ship.*

*If Byzantine boatswains were responsible for the ship's boat,
then the grapnel stowed aft of the galley is evidence of a kind that
Georgios' crew included a boatswain, who also would have been
responsible for rigging and cables.*

As for ordinary seamen who may have served on board, we can-

*not guess. In American days of sail, square-rigged ships only
slightly smaller than Georgios' merchantman often had a crew of
no more than three men and a boy. There may not have been many
ordinary seamen in the crew to eat further into the profits from the
venture. Indeed, there may have been none.*

*Whether or not parascharites stands for cook, there was cer-
tainly a cook aboard the ship. The cramped galley in which he
worked was located at the extreme stern, set as low as possible
within the hull, and had an overall floor area of barely three and
a half by nine feet. The galley had a deckhouse superstructure
roofed with tiles, including one tile with a circular hole that was
intended to let the smoke from the galley fire escape. The precise
arrangement of the hearth where the fire burned is not reconstructed with certainty. It was built of tiles and iron bars, and it
stood in the port half of the galley. Perhaps its tiles formed a low
firebox, open at the top and covered by a grill of iron rods that
supported the round-bottomed pots used for cooking.*

*The cook had at his disposal twenty-two such pots, stowed near
the hearth. Elsewhere in the galley, on shelves and perhaps also in
the galley's forward locker, was a quantity of dining wares.
Georgios was evidently not laggard in the fashions of the day: four
of his bowls are the oldest precisely dated examples of Byzantine
lead-glazed pottery. Besides these there were eight plain red plates
or dishes, two cups, three jars with spouts (two with lids), and
eighteen pitchers. Most of the pitchers were coated inside with
resin, which indicates that they were used to hold wine. A further
array of seventeen storage jars of various shapes and sizes, doubt-
less including one or two filled with lamp oil, and possibly the
ship's large water jar, were kept on the starboard side of the galley.*

*The galley also contained a number of copper pitchers and a
copper tray, a stone mortar and pestle, a millstone, a whetstone, a
spoon with leaden bowl, and three steelyards. More valuable items,
including a supply of money, a set of balance-pan weights, glass-
ware, and a bronze censer with wick pin (possibly for providing
incense after meals or for sanctifying the ship as we know was
done in more recent times), were most likely stored in the galley's
forward locker.*

*The coarser jugs and pitchers and three copper cauldrons were
stowed in a storage section at the very stern of the galley. It was
here that were kept the grapnel, fishing gear, and, clearly separated*

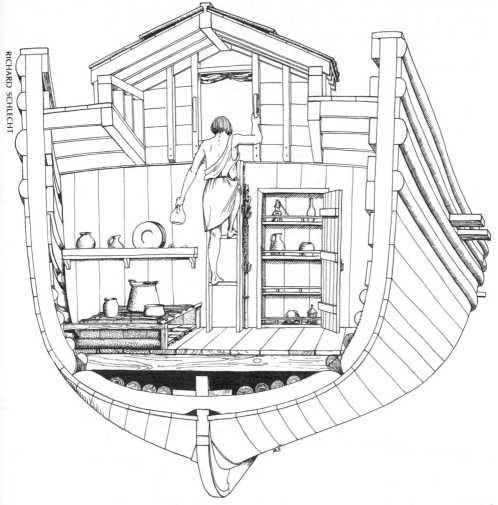

from the carpenter's kit, another group of iron tools: axes, a pick-axe, pruning hooks, and a shovel. These look like boatswain's stores that would have been needed by a landing party to collect firewood for the cook and to enlarge springs to obtain fresh water.

Lastly there were three bronze belt buckles and a metal belt-tip sheath, hopefully only from a change of clothing.

What can be said about the ship's last voyage? We have noted that Georgios, in addition to being the captain, may have been the owner and a merchant–venturer as well. The basis for this conjecture is the fact that the scale bearing his name is an item of merchant's equipment. It should be mentioned that later Venetian statutes required that ship owners supply every vessel with a weighing device; perhaps even during Byzantine times a captain, merchant or not, may have needed to carry his own balance to show that his freight charges were correct. If we may assume, however, that Georgios was the owner as well as master, we can calculate with some confidence his total investment in the ship and all its stores.

The Rhodian sea law indicates that the seventh-century cost of fully outfitted shipping ran about fifty solidi (gold coins) per six and a half tons' capacity. On this basis Georgios' investment would have been some four hundred and sixty solidi, a substantial sum in times when a shipyard caulker might earn eighteen solidi for a year's work and less skilled laborers might receive only seven or eight. Might this investment have been all Georgios could afford, leaving him with no capital to invest in a cargo? A shipload of wine, for example, would have cost two hundred or three hundred solidi more at current prices. One piece of evidence suggests that such was the case.

A single lead seal on board bears a cross-shaped monogram that we read as the name Iannes, or John. Such a seal could of course have belonged to a passenger or crew member—it may even have been only a button—but the possibility exists of its being for official use. Perhaps John was the emporos, or merchant, aboard Georgios' ship, traveling with him to pay the freight charge and handle the sale of goods at the vessel's destination.

If John was indeed a merchant or merchant's agent, he would have been required by law to ask other merchants who had sailed with Georgios whether or not the ship was in good condition. When he had heard that it was, he and Georgios would have entered into a contract. Just where John or his employer had raised the money to buy a cargo was no one else's affair as long as he could pay Georgios the required freight charge.

We can visualize next a procession of porters carrying aboard the cargo of nine-hundred-odd amphoras and passing them down through the hatch into the hold. Most of the storage jars were large and globular but some were smaller and more elongated. The large jars would hold as much as forty liters of liquid, the small ones *around nine liters. We cannot be sure what, if anything, the jars contained. Not all of them were lined with resin, the customary method of waterproofing the porous clay. However, if all the jars had been filled with liquid, say wine, the cargo would have weighed some thirty-seven tons.*

The cook's stores would have been loaded at the same time. Presumably he saw to it that his large jar had been filled with fresh water and checked his supply of lamp oil. We know that his fresh rations included a basketful of dark, gleaming Bosphorus mussels; their empty shells, carefully nested within one another, were later set aside for some unknown use.

The prow officer—if such was his responsibility—lashed a pair of anchors to the port gunwale and another to the starboard gunwale near the bow and stacked the remaining seven just forward of the mast. The ship was under way.

Although there is no archaeological evidence for it, we may assume, from seventh-century practice, that port taxes had been paid, and that they soon passed a customs point where they were charged export duty.

Meanwhile the captain had placed in the galley certain valuables, including a money purse or two. These held at least fifty-four copper folles (coins worth a small fraction of a solidus) and sixteen small gold pieces; the total value of the coins was just a little more than seven solidi. Was this a ship's fund or money deposited by a passenger? The Rhodian sea law declares: "If a passenger comes on board and has gold, let him deposit it with the captain. If he does not deposit it and says 'I have lost gold or silver,' no effect is to be given to what he says, since he did not deposit it with the captain." If one is to try to answer the question, one needs to know something about the purchasing power of the solidus.

As we have noted, seven solidi represented a year's wage for some kinds of labor; early in the eighth century, for example, a blacksmith earned three-quarters of a solidus per month. Early in the seventh century a cloak might cost from one to three solidi, and later in the century one solidus would buy four cheap blankets. Food was much less dear. One sixth-century figure gives five solidi as the cost of a year's rations for one man; in the years when our ship made its final voyage a loaf of bread cost three folles. The money found in the purses would have fed a crew of fifteen for a month with something left over, not even taking into considera-

tion the evidence (lead weights for fishing lines and nets) that the ship's company supplemented its provisions en route. It therefore seems likely that the contents of the purse or purses were the ship's victualing money. With port and customs taxes already paid, there would have been no need to risk more cash at sea.

The seventy coins enable us today to pinpoint the date of the voyage at A.D. 625 or 626. Six of the coins were too badly preserved to allow identification. Of the remainder only two were minted earlier than the reign of the Emperor Heraclius (A.D. 610–641). The latest coin in the group was minted in the sixteenth year of the emperor's reign, that is in A.D. 625/626. We may safely assume that the ship last sailed in the same year or quite soon thereafter.

The weighing equipment for the voyage was also stowed in the galley cupboard or close to it. The balance-pan weights, made of bronze inlaid with silver, came in a wooden tray that held them in a graduated series in cylindrical pockets. Seven of the original nine weights were recovered. In addition we found what may be a fragment of the balance itself. The bronze steelyard beam that bears Georgios' name was one of three scales of this kind on board; one of the other two was made of iron and was therefore poorly preserved.

Georgios' steelyard beam is decorated with a boar's head at one end and the head of another animal, possibly a dog or lion, at the other. It has two fulcrum points and two calibrated scales, for heavy or light loads; the counterweight is a lead-filled bust of the goddess Athena, similar to those carried on ships lost off Sicily and in the Bosphorus during the same period.

Both bronze steelyard beams are calibrated in terms of a pound that was equal to 315 grams (our pound troy, which is 375 grams, is the closest modern equivalent; our pound avoirdupois is 453 grams), seemingly the same lightweight pound used as the unit of measurement for the ship's anchors. The same unit is very close to one determined earlier from weights of fifth-century and sixth-century Byzantine times.

Curiously the balance-pan weights represent an entirely different system. Most are clearly marked; they include a 1-litra, or 1-pound, weight; a 6-unciae, or 6-ounce weight, and 3-ounce, 2-ounce, and 1-ounce weights. Two smaller weights are unmarked: one of 3 nomismata (6 nomismata normally equaled 1 uncia) and the other of 1 nomisma. This is possibly the most complete set of Byzantine weights in existence, and their pound is not the standard "light" 315-gram one. It is superlight: 287 grams. Furthermore, it is a pound divided into 14 ounces rather than the customary 12, and its ounce is divided into 7 nomismata rather than 6.

These unusual values are not the result of any alteration in the original weights as a consequence of their long submersion. Each of the weights in the set, give or take a fraction of a gram, is consistent with all the others; in every case the ounce is 20.45 grams. It happens that an ounce of this weight was the Byzantine standard for gold coinage; the standard was established in the time of Constantine the Great (A.D. 272–337) on the basis of the old Roman pound (327.45 grams). In this coinage-weight system, however, there were 16 ounces to the pound rather than 14. Only one other 14-ounce pound is known: during the fourth century a "heavy" pound divided into 14 ounces rather than 12 was used in the mining of gold in order to increase state revenues from mine leases. All of this, however, can have nothing to do with the standard of the balance-pan weights on the ship. At present it remains unexplained.

The ship carried one more balance weight. It is a small pendant of yellow glass that is pierced for stringing. It is so similar in appearance to other Byzantine glass weights that it must have been one. The pendant is shaped like a coin, and pressed into the glass is another cruciform monogram; this one gives the name Theodoros. Such weights are thought to have been used to check gold coins, although the weights of the glass pieces seldom correspond to the weights of any coins then in circulation. The discrepancy is explained on the grounds that the glass pieces have lost weight as a result of corrosion.

The ship sailed southward along the western coast of Asia Minor, her square sail swelled by the following meltem. Halicarnassus was only a few hours away.

The helmsman steered a course that would keep him as near the small, flat island as he felt was safe. From his low ship he could not see the change of color in the water ahead. Whitecaps camouflaged the breakers in their midst. The ship drew nearer the reef, pitching rhythmically. Her bows rose and fell, again and again until, at last, they plunged into a watery trough whose bottom was solid rock.

The helmsman probably tried to steer directly for the island, little more than a hundred yards away. But already his stricken *vessel was under the lee of its shore. Her sails fell slack. She lost way in deep water less than a hundred yards from the shallow bottom on which she might have settled.*

Planing this way and that, like a falling leaf, she silently drifted downward. She landed on an even keel, still pointing toward the island, and then listed to port. Shipworms began their relentless attack on her unprotected starboard side. In which year did the starboard anchors, held high above the seabed, break free and drop to the sand? When did the hearth tiles fall to the tilting galley floor, and slide into a heap along its port edge? For how many years did the mast stand?

We have seen Georgios' ship built, supplied, loaded, under way, and lost. What can we say of its course and its intended destination?

It seems safe to state, on the basis of the coins alone, that the voyage was from north to south. All the identifiable coins but one, a very early coin from Alexandretta *ad Issum* on what is now the Levantine coast of Turkey, were minted in the north: at Constantinople, Thessalonica, Nicomedia, and Cyzicus. Although these were major mints whose coins might be found in any ship, their overwhelmingly northern location suggests that the home port of the ship should probably be sought in the same direction.

The pottery from the galley strengthens this assumption. Fully half the lamps are Asia Minor types, with their best parallels coming from Ephesus, Miletus, Samos, Smyrna, Troy, and Delos; similar lamps have also been found on Chios. Seven of the lamps are of a type common to western Bulgaria, Rumania, Thrace, and the Hellespont. In Rumania, at least, archaeologists are divided as to whether they are local products or imports into the Black Sea. A number of counterparts for this type exist also from excavations in Constantinople, but there, too, there is a question of origin. The remainder of the two dozen lamps cannot yet be assigned a provenance, but, as with the coins, none of them seems to have come from west, south, or east of the point where the ship sank.

Other wares from the galley also find their best parallels to the north. The lead-glazed bowls speak of Constantinople, and other pottery is similar to the ware of Chios and of two Black Sea ports: Histria and Tomis. The plain red plates are believed to be African in origin, but such plates were so popular and widely spread in the Mediterranean as to have been available almost anywhere.

All of these clues, based on similarities in pottery, depend on the fortunes of excavation and publication; some of the best parallels were excavated within the preceding few years, changing tentative conclusions we had reached in the early 1960s when our study began.

Two clues to the route of the ship remain. First, the mussels were most probably taken on somewhere near the Bosphorus. Second, the ship, beyond any reasonable doubt, was sailing in a southeasterly direction before a *meltem* wind when it hit the reef at Yassi Ada, tore a hole in its bottom, and sank almost immediately on the southeast side of the reef.

The ship's cargo and destination is less certain. Many of the amphoras in its cargo were lined with resin, indicating at least a partial cargo of wine. The ship was sailing toward Cos, Cnidus, and Rhodes, all wine-producing centers, but it may have carried some special wine from the north, perhaps from Thasos where a similar type of amphora is well known from excavations.

The best parallels for all of the amphora types in the cargo are to be found in sites along the western coast of the Black Sea. There they are considered to be imports from some unknown region. The amphoras, which held resins, iron nails, and pigments at the Tomis chandlery, were similar, but not identical, to those on the ship; the slight differences are perhaps explained by their slightly earlier date. Is there a region that exported these products, as well as wine? Or were old wine containers simply reused for shipping other materials after their original contents had been drained.

There is, perhaps, another explanation. Today one sees vessels plying the Aegean whose hold and deck are crowded with pottery containers. The pots are empty; they are the cargo. The rather large number of tile-carrying and plate-carrying shipwrecks in the Mediterranean, some from the Byzantine period, prove that other ceramic products were shipped rather than fabricated where needed. Is it not plausible that empty amphoras were also shipped from manufacturing centers, in this case perhaps Constantinople, where many fragments of our types have been excavated. There is supporting evidence for this:

Only a hundred or so amphora stoppers were found for the nine-hundred-odd amphoras in the ship (admittedly, the remaining stoppers could have been of perishable material).

It is not illogical to suggest that Georgios was carrying a load of the best wine jars available on the Constantinople (or Black Sea) pottery market for the use of vintners in the south, and that the merchant John had decided to cut costs a little by having some of the unlined pots coated with resin on the voyage. A cargo of empty amphoras would have been light, but as sand was sometimes used as ballast, we have no way of knowing how heavily ballasted the ship was, nor how much ballast might have gone up our air-lift tube.

CHAPTER X
Gadgets

THE excavation of the Byzantine ship had cost $100,000. It had taken a total of 3,533 individual dives by a dozen divers. We had spent 1,243 man-hours on the seabed in 211 diving days.

On land, five people working normal eight-hour days could have done the same job in just one month.

For the excavation of the Roman ship at Yassi Ada, to begin in 1967, I wanted greater efficiency. It was about the same size as the Byzantine wreck. If we could excavate it in only two summers rather than four, we might halve such annual expenses as transportation, rental of local boats, salaries, setting up camp, shipping, insurance, and customs.

Fred made an efficiency study of the diving logs to determine how we had spent our time on the Byzantine wreck. Removal of sand and shell had taken 694 hours, or 64% of the total; of this, 224 hours were spent air-lifting and 470 hours sweeping sand away by hand. Making plans by photography and drawing consumed 204 hours, or 19% of our time. Removal of amphoras, anchors, and small finds took 115 hours, or 11% of the time, and bringing up hull remains 41 hours, or 4%. The remaining 2%, or 24 hours, was used to anchor the barge, pin wood in place, and cover the wreck with sand at the end of each season. He did not count about 160 hours of "unnecessary" work—making a documentary film and taking photographs for popular articles.

I saw two approaches to reducing the number of summers required for the job. First, by increasing the number of divers and making longer dives we might be able to log 1,200 hours in two campaigns rather than four, even though the Roman wreck, at 120 to 140 feet, lay deeper than the Byzantine ship. Second, by accomplishing more on each dive, we might be able to reduce necessary man-hours on the seabed. Both would require new equipment and techniques.

I decided to follow both approaches, realizing that the initial cost of each season would be greater than before. I spent the winter adapting and designing tools for the job, picking the brains of Michael, Susan, Fred, and Don during long sessions in my office. Our new gadgets included:

- A submersible decompression chamber to allow longer dives.
- A high-pressure water jet to wash away the bulk of sand overburden.
- A large track-mounted air lift to suck up sand cleared from the wreck.
- An improved stereophotogrammetric mapping system for the *Asherah.*
- A basket that could raise half a ton of cargo, or twenty to thirty amphoras at a time, to the surface with a lifting balloon.
- An underwater telephone booth to improve communications.
- An underwater detector to pinpoint metal objects beneath sand.
- A large four-man, double-lock recompression chamber for treatment of any diving illness.
- We would also have the use of Mehmet Turguttekin's new sixty-five-foot trawler *Kardeshler,* specially designed to be used for fishing in winters and archaeology in summers; her cabin was placed forward to provide ample deck space for diving and lowering equipment.

Financial support came again from the University Museum, the National Geographic Society, the National Science Foundation, and Nixon Griffis, with an additional grant from the Triopian Foundation for Archaeological Research. Our new recompression chamber was paid for largely by the Rockefeller Foundation. We were also backed by funds and equipment from the United States Navy, to perfect our methods of mapping from a submarine, and to evaluate several types of side-scanning sonar we planned to use in a concurrent survey for much deeper wrecks.

I had met Dr. J.B. Hersey of the Office of Naval Research, and Captain W.F. Searle, Supervisor of Salvage, at a symposium on the use of research submarines. The meeting led to support from their offices, as well as from the Deep Submergence Systems Project, Naval Oceanographic Office, and Naval Research Laboratory. I asked Captain Searle if navy support of archaeology didn't seem a little strange.

"One of our jobs is to find wrecks and planes lost at sea, and then to survey them before bringing up the pieces to be put back together for study," he answered. "You're doing the same thing and working on some of the same problems. The only difference is that your wrecks went down hundreds or thousands of years earlier."

To increase the staff I needed about twenty-five strong, rugged divers. One hundred forty feet is the limit at which the navy allows its highly trained Underwater Demolition Team divers to work without the exigency of military need.

I asked for volunteers from my graduate seminar in Ancient Seafaring: Marilyn Rosenberg, Marie Ryan, Cynthia Jones, Nancy Palmer, and Karen Vitelli raised their hands. Only one had dived before. They enrolled in a YMCA course along with other students, including several men.

My shoes were dusted with bright yellow pollen from a surprising blanket of April wild flowers as I walked to the top of Yassi Ada at the beginning of the 1967 season. In previous years on the island I had seldom ventured beyond our tiny beachhead on the water's edge. Now the foundations of a new village (population forty-five) spread below me. Quarters for men and women were being raised, walls for a workhouse were under construction, green tents ran in a row along the crest of the island, and the concrete floor for a darkroom was being poured. Mehmet had earlier dynamited away part of the low cliff opposite the wreck site, to form a platform for our recompression chamber.

Architect Matt Kaplan had come to Bodrum a month earlier with Claude, who arranged for boats, barge, and equipment. Not know-

Yassi Ada, population forty-five of us, in 1967. The barge is moored over the Roman wreck; the Kardeshler *is nearby, and the* Asherah *close to shore.*

ing a word of Turkish, Matt had sailed to Yassi Ada with ten local workmen to construct our settlement, and had not spoken English for weeks. He already managed well in his new tongue, but had worked himself to exhaustion and collapsed with a raging fever soon after my arrival. Our new colonists, men and women together, joined in, hauling rocks and sawing lumber to complete the job by mid-May. The hardest task was to get the three-ton recompression chamber from the *Kardeshler* to the island without heavy lifting gear, but Mehmet and his crew accomplished it with the patience of pyramid-builders, using jacks, pipe rollers, ramps and block and tackle.

During these preparations a sudden storm tore the barge from temporary moorings near the spot where we unloaded equipment onto our rocky coast. Claude was still in Bodrum. Oktay Ercan, who had taken me for my first open-water dive in the Bosphorus years before, was the only other experienced diver among us. Together we swam through the waves, dived and repaired the broken cables.

Preparations for an underwater excavation. The author watches the arrival at Yassi Ada of tons of equipment needed for a successful summer.

We could scarcely pull our tired bodies up the rubber-tire fenders of the barge when we finished. Nearly twenty people had watched our struggle from the island, unable to lend a hand, for none had ever made a single dive outside a swimming pool. Yet, four months later, joined by Claude, Eric, Michael, Susan, and other old hands, we had made more than 1,700 dives without mishap.

Once excavation was under way our submersible decompression chamber (SDC) permitted us to make longer dives than before, although the new site was deeper than the old. We had in the past been limited by the maximum amount of time we could reasonably decompress in the open sea—about twenty-five minutes twice a day —which would allow little more than half an hour of working time, in two dives, at the deep end of the Roman wreck. Sometimes we had decompressed longer, but it was not pleasant, even after the discovery that pocketbooks last for weeks under water. A bucket filled with a compost of old westerns and mysteries then dangled at the ten-foot stop where, hanging to a rope like a commuter to a subway strap, I was able to finish Norman Mailer's *The Deer Park* before its pages reverted to pulp.

With our submersible decompression chamber—basically a sphere with an entry hatch in its bottom—up to four divers could now decompress for long periods in warm, dry comfort while still under water. The sphere was filled with fresh air through a hose from a compressor on Yassi Ada, sixty yards away. Inside we read and played chess or an insane brand of soccer dubbed "idiotball."

We could talk by telephone to a "switchboard operator," usually Larry, on the island. From his post near the recompression chamber there, he could communicate also with the barge by handi-talkie radio, and those on the barge could relay messages to divers on the wreck by means of the underwater telephone booth. The communications network provided instant contact between all staff members in case of emergency.

Necessity had dictated the specifications of our SDC. Knowing we would have no large support ship to raise and lower it, I had designed it to be independent of surface vessels. Its depth, and therefore its pressure, was regulated by a cable running from it to a pulley on the seabed and then on up to a winch on Yassi Ada. One man on the island could let the divers up through the various stages of decompression, ten feet at a time, the interior pressure always being the same as that at the level of the open bottom hatch.

In the event that a diver should get the bends during decompression I had designed a lock on the side of the sphere through which a victim could be placed into our old one-man portable chamber and carried to land, still under pressure, to be locked into the big recompression chamber. In theory the idea was sound, but we were glad not to test it. The SDC was also capable of being sealed, taken from the water, and mated with the land-based recompression chamber, where the patient could receive medical treatment; with no crane to lift the whole thing onto land, however, this was only a feature for possible future use.

For some days after the SDC was in place we were afraid to use it. The upward pull of a six-and-a-half-foot sphere filled with air is tremendous. Even though the pulley on the seabed was attached to five tons of metal ballast, the surge of surface wave action on rough

A diver swims up into our submersible decompression chamber (SDC) after working 140 feet deep on the Roman wreck. The depth of the air-filled sphere is controlled by cables that run to a pulley on the seabed and then up to the boat.

JOHN CASSILS

days jerked the cable hard enough to raise the ballast several inches off the bottom. We were not sure how long the cable would take successive tugs. If the cable broke, we feared the SDC would shoot to the surface, killing the divers inside by rupturing their lungs with the sudden drop in pressure.

We tested this theory through my own blunder. In order to change one of its cables, Ben Jones and I flooded the SDC and sank it to the bottom. After finishing the job, we began to refill the sphere with air so that it would rise again to the surface. Then it could be winched down to the required depth.

I had simply shoved the air hose up through the bottom hatch. Just as the great yellow ball began to budge on the ocean floor, I decided to pull it out. I swam to the chamber, thrust my head and shoulders up into it, and tried to free the hose. It was tangled. I pulled as hard as I could, but it would not come free. I stayed a second too long.

Hanging out of the hatch, I felt the sudden rush of water against my legs and realized that the chamber was rising rapidly, carrying me toward the surface. As the sphere rose through the water, the air inside expanded, making it ever more buoyant. We gathered speed and rushed upward like a missile.

Just as we hit the surface I pushed downward with all my strength, tumbling backward and out. A ton of auxiliary ballast, bolted to the cable just a few feet below the sphere, shot by my head, missing me by inches.

I was furious with myself. I would have been furious if any of the other divers had been so stupid. I was also scared. With my eyes closed I rolled into a still ball and let myself sink back to the bottom. I knelt in the mud, wondering if I had burst a lung, waiting for a sign of blood or pain. I did not know if I had breathed out on the way up, the only way to prevent a rupture.

Ben swam over and asked me with his hands if I was all right. I must have exhaled, unconsciously, for I felt no ill effects. I made an O.K. sign with my fingers and sheepishly joined him in collecting wrenches, screwdrivers, and cable clamps lying where we had worked.

We moved our rusting scaffold of angle-iron "step frames" from the barren scar where the Byzantine wreck had been and erected them over the mound of amphoras that marked the Roman wreck. Then, like submarine gandy dancers, we laid seventy feet of "railroad track" along the lower side of the new site. The track was made of a pair of overhead industrial monorails, turned upside down and kept parallel by wooden ties. Our new aluminum air lift, ten inches in diameter, was pierced by a pipe axle fastened to wheeled trolleys at either end. The trolleys were designed to hang from overhead

The large air lift used in 1967 was moved along seventy feet of underwater "railroad track" placed along the deeper edge of the wreck. Paul Fardig here removes a mound of sand that had been forced down from the wreck with our water jet.

tracks in factories, to carry heavy loads from place to place. Now they too were inverted so that the air lift "hung" upward, buoyed at the top by an air-filled oil drum.

Pairs of divers moved the air lift along the edge of the site, sucking up mountains of sand accumulating beneath the tracks from our water jet. With the jet, a fire hose with "kick free" nozzle, we removed tons of sand overburden, finding that by using a fogging nozzle we could get quite close to fragile wood without disturbing it.

The stream from a high-pressure water jet carries sand from the Roman wreck off to one side of the site. Part of the metal scaffolding that supported our photo towers is seen already assembled and leveled.

JOHN CASSILS

On the other, upper side of the wreck stood the underwater "telephone booth," the brainchild of Michael and Susan, a Plexiglas hemisphere attached to 1,500 pounds of steel plate ballast by angle-iron legs. As many as four divers could stand inside, dry from their chests up, breathing air pumped into the dome from the barge.

Our entrapped air bubble was meant as a communications center. Teams of divers discussed problems with each other and, by telephone, with others on the barge. Once, as a *tour de force*, we placed a transceiver radio by the barge telephone so that Matt Kaplan at his drawing board on Yassi Ada could talk directly to a diver looking out over the wreck Matt drew.

The phone booth also served as a refuge, and it was for that purpose that it later was adopted by the Tektite project and other programs using underwater habitats, where divers live for days beneath the sea to avoid frequent decompression and need way stations during excursions away from home. Such divers become saturated with compressed gases from the air they breathe so that decompression at the end of their stay, although taking many hours, will be the same at the end of three days or three weeks.

In midsummer I was cleaning sand from some wood fragments when I felt a hand on my shoulder. I looked up and saw Gail Hillard run her index finger across her throat, the sign she was out of air. It was 135 feet to the surface, but with three kicks of her flippers she was breathing fresh air inside the dome. I followed her in.

"I ran out of air," she said calmly, "and my reserve didn't work."

I took her mouthpiece and tested it. "I think you've got enough to get to the hoses at the decompression stop. I'll stick close by, so if you can't make it we can share my air. Let's go."

We could have telephoned the surface and had an extra tank sent down, but it wasn't necessary. Afterward we kept an emergency tank in the booth at all times. More than once it averted possible panic.

A spear gun was also propped in the booth. Morays poked their heads sporadically from amphora necks, their sharp teeth threatening us as they moved their mouths in the hideous jawing movement peculiar to the species. The morays never reappeared in the same jars, and we became hesitant about putting our hands into the cargo. Eric, who had never speared anything in his life, took a shot at one, succeeding only in wounding it. In an instant the eel was on him, thrashing and bumping against his body as the two of them desperately tried to escape one another.

The telephone booth, a clear plastic hemisphere on metal legs, situated near the Roman wreck. Fresh air is brought into the dome by hose from a compressor on the diving barge above. The entrapped air bubble allows a diver to stand inside, dry from his chest up, and talk by telephone to the barge.

JOHN CASSILS

A sharp-toothed moray watches menacingly from the mouth of an amphora in the Roman cargo. Morays also liked to hide under the telephone booth.

MARTIN KLEIN

Other, less dangerous creatures also lived in the amphoras. Ben Jones caught an octopus for dinner, and finished his half-hour dive with the writhing mollusk zipped inside his rubber jacket. He claimed it was delicious that night, but his chest was covered with a pox of red circles from a hundred suction cups.

Most dives were no more exciting than commuting to an office. An "adventurous" dive usually indicates human error, which we tried to keep to a minimum. Our most frightening experience had nothing to do with diving.

The July sky was clear azure as I dropped over the side of the barge. When I returned to the surface forty minutes later I asked where the world had gone. The Turkish mainland had vanished, and nearby islands were barely visible. The sky had turned an ugly black. From the south we heard the sound of a long sigh, and saw a jagged white sea spreading toward us like a flash flood racing through a valley.

The storm closed in with incredible speed. There were divers decompressing whom we could not leave, but I sent most of the crew to Yassi Ada. Before they reached the shore, wind and rain struck.

The sea, white foam on dark grey water, looked unreal, like the unconvincing waves shot in studio tanks for low-budget pirate films. Even the howling wind seemed artificial to me.

A typical day on the diving barge. Even in mid-summer the cold meltem *wind kept staff members huddled for warmth behind canvas flaps.*

BENNETT JONES

The lightning, though, was real. It stalked us, flashing first through the clouds in the direction of mainland mountains, then striking in succession the island peaks between the mainland and Yassi Ada. We stood and shivered in the pouring rain, uncomfortably aware that we were the highest objects on the barge. As the bolts came nearer, Terry Cummer, one of my students, wanted to swim ashore. I advised against it.

The blinding flash and earsplitting crack were simultaneous—a burst of light and sound. The smell of ozone thickened the air. Marilyn Rosenberg, from the island, saw it hit. The lightning had struck sixty feet from us, between the barge and the island, just where Terry might have been.

The storm moved away as rapidly as it had appeared.

We had planned to photograph each stage of the excavation from the *Asherah,* but she was delayed and arrived halfway through the summer. We fell back on our old technique and built a new photo tower to map the cargo as we removed it.

The first wood emerged from the sand, bits of ceiling—or inner hull lining—sticking to solid ribs. Beneath the ribs were the strakes, or rows of outer hull planks. All were much better preserved than on the Byzantine ship.

Each day we hoped we would come upon the ship's galley. There we expected to find small articles that would date accurately the merchant vessel's last voyage; her amphoras, longer than those on the Byzantine ship and with knobs on their bottoms, suggested only a vague date in the fifth or sixth century for her sinking.

Finally we thought we had found a clue. Tableware began to appear. But it was covered with bright green glaze—unlike any Roman pottery we had ever seen. Could our dating of the amphoras be so far wrong?

Adding to our bewilderment, some of the timbers we uncovered ran off at an oblique angle from the rest of the ship. Only slowly did we realize that this was a second, more recent, wreck lying under the sand, and lying directly on top of the Roman hulk. We guessed, erroneously, that the pottery was of the thirteenth or fourteenth century; a coin of Philip III of Spain, found during a later season, pointed to the early seventeenth.

I asked Yüksel if he would direct the excavation of the new wreck. Tracing its hull away from the Roman ship, he found that it almost reached the spot where the Byzantine ship had rested. Three ships, centuries apart, had ripped their bottoms on Yassi Ada's reef and settled virtually on top of one another.

Our staff was so large that camp life lacked the closeness of previous summers. Thursday-night parties seemed forced. Michael and Susan had to spend more time in Izmir, handling the logistics of getting each piece of equipment through customs and shipped to us, than they could on Yassi Ada. David Owen was studying archaeology in Turkey on a Fulbright fellowship and came only briefly—in answer to my telegram saying simply "Help"—to put together the assortment of pipes and fittings, air tanks, air conditioner, compressor, gauges, and thermometers that came with the big recompression chamber. He returned almost immediately to his cuneiform tablets in Ankara.

Old-timers Claude and Oktay moved out of the crowded men's dormitory to build their own bachelor quarters, in the style of a Tahitian hut Claude had seen somewhere. In spare moments they leveled a site, collected scrap lumber around the camp, and brought reed mats out to the island.

"We don't want any slums on Yassi Ada," I said, poking fun at the "tar-paper shack" which would blight our community. Someone suggested laying spare track from the air lift across their end of the island so we could refer to the "wrong side of the tracks."

But the reed hut became the coolest and most popular spot on the island. Every afternoon its mat floor was covered by sleeping divers trying to escape the oppressive heat of their tents during siesta. Evenings we sat around a giant samovar in the middle of the lamp-lit room, talking and listening to Claude practice his *saz,* a long-handled string instrument popular in Turkey.

Not everyone could stop to talk after sunset. Photographs were developed and printed daily, and the darkroom generator now ran far into the night. Plans of the Roman ship's cargo were being completed and inked, showing how amphoras had been stacked in the ancient hold. We remained disappointed throughout the summer, however, that we did not find the ship's galley.

The arrival of the *Asherah* from Izmir, her new coat of red paint gleaming from *Kardeshler*'s deck, buoyed our spirits until the question struck home: how could we unload a five-ton submarine when there was no crane within a hundred miles able to lift half that weight?

We considered sailing under a bridge, hooking the *Asherah* from above, and sailing out from under her. There were no bridges close by. We looked, without success, for a large cave to serve the same purpose.

The *Kardeshler* sailed into Bodrum harbor and tied up by the only other trawler. Each had a boom able to lift two tons. In tandem they hoisted the submarine a few feet off the deck, their masts and booms shivering under the strain.

It was the only time I have seen Mehmet defeated by a heavy load. He and the other captain tried to swing the *Asherah* out over the water, but found it impossible to maneuver their booms. When they had worked the submarine into a position from which she could no longer be lowered back onto the deck, I saw one of the steel booms begin to buckle. I turned my back to avoid seeing the inevitable. The submarine crashed onto *Kardeshler*'s gunwale, knocking a large hole in her Fiberglas tail. She sat there for another week, hanging half out over the water, while we sought individual solutions to the problem.

Claude looked for telephone poles he proposed binding together to form a giant tripod from which he would lift the *Asherah* with a series of chain hoists.

Yüksel approached the captain of a large freighter anchored just outside the harbor, but the captain refused to take responsibility for lifting an object not on his orders.

I discussed our problem with the officers of an American destroyer on a goodwill visit in Bodrum. They wanted to help, but had nothing on board that could raise five tons.

Finally a large Turkish freighter arrived in Bodrum, and its captain consented to lift the submarine with his crane. The *Asherah* stayed in the water for the rest of the summer, anchored like a rowboat off Yassi Ada when not in operation, until the freighter repeated its assistance on a return trip.

Don Rosencrantz was in charge of the *Asherah* again, on leave from Lockheed where he was now an engineer on a deep diving rescue submarine being built for the navy. He had designed and built an improved mapping system for us.

As Don and Yüksel passed back and forth over the wreck in the submarine, two motorized cameras with specially ground underwater lenses were triggered simultaneously with a pair of strobo-

Matt Kaplan and Ben Jones prepare stereo cameras to be mounted on the Asherah, *anchored between Yassi Ada and the trawler* Kardeshler.

CHARLES R. NICKLIN, JR.

Stereo-pairs of the Roman hull taken from the Asherah. *An internal camera simultaneously photographed a control panel for use in analysis.*

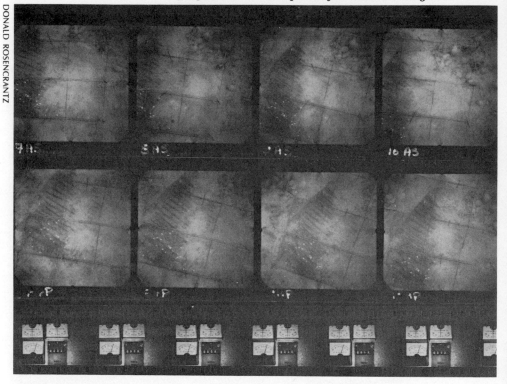

DONALD ROSENCRANTZ

scopic lights. Closed-circuit television served as a viewfinder for the system, allowing them to see on a monitor inside what was directly beneath the cameras outside. An interior camera provided a permanent record of each "flight" over the wreck, automatically photographing a counter and tilt and depth indicators whenever a stereophoto was taken.

Yüksel's role as submarine pilot was in many ways his simplest. His main duty, as government representative, was to see that our work was not only competent, but above suspicion in a land suffering a disturbing number of antiquities thefts, many from wrecks. He advised me daily about seemingly innocent acts that might lead to harmful rumors.

I tried to cooperate. My staff dived only at Yassi Ada. Even there we made exploratory dives away from the vicinity of the wreck only if Yüksel accompanied us. He was not on the daily diving roster so that he could dive, unannounced, with any team he chose to follow and inspect. I asked local captains not to bring tourists to the island without first getting permission from the Bodrum Museum. None of us boarded foreign yachts without him.

It was an awkward situation for both of us. At the risk of offending me, he warned me about being seen with this or that person in Bodrum.

"He does not have a good reputation," he would say.

"He just asked me to have coffee with him."

He felt I was too trusting of others; I thought he was too suspicious. In retrospect, I realize that his judgment was almost always correct. He kept our reputation spotless, although there were days that made his job nearly impossible:

On a routine mapping mission over the wreck, the *Asherah* was turned sideways by a violent current and swept far out past the reef toward Greek waters. We lost underwater contact, but through binoculars from the island I saw her surface about a mile away. A Greek gunboat, perhaps by chance, appeared from behind the Greek island of Kalymnos.

"I hope you're carrying your passport, Yüksel, so you won't be shot as a spy," I radioed cheerfully. He did not think it was funny.

The "Ahmet Express," a decrepit fishing boat we used to bring fresh water, bread, and a few other staples from nearby villages, gave chase and threw a line. The feeble boat and the submarine were swept farther to sea.

As the *Kardeshler* weighed anchor to go to the rescue, strange ships entered the usually barren seascape. The Greek warship drew closer as a large ketch with Panamanian flag approached under full sail. Before either reached the sub, a powerful British speedboat, hull as white as the tall wake she threw up behind her, roared into view from the north.

I knew the captain of the speedboat, but Yüksel had earlier told me he didn't want it near Yassi Ada. Speedboats are used to smuggle antiquities, and villagers watching from Karatoprak on the coast might well conclude we were up to no good. Drifting farther toward Greece, Yüksel refused a line from the speedboat and waited for *Kardeshler* to arrive and tow him back to the island.

Yüksel was more than upset. "Why did that speedboat come here when I was down in the submarine?" he asked me with annoyance.

I protested that I had nothing to do with it. I hoped the affair might soon be forgotten when, only hours later, Yüksel entered the workhouse enraged.

"Who are those divers? Just what is your idea? What are you trying to do?"

In disbelief I saw two black-suited divers, gleaming wet with tanks on their backs, crawling up the rocks on the far side of Yassi Ada.

I had never seen either before. They said they were tourists, abandoned by the boat that had taken them diving. Even I was unconvinced. By their accents we guessed them to be German or Austrian. Shortly afterward a fisherman picked them up, and we never saw them again—the following week they were found dead on the floor of the sea near Bodrum. The death remains a mystery surrounded by local gossip.

The atmosphere was still tense when we went to bed that evening. Near midnight, Yüksel ran from his tent to mine.

"George, just what *is* going on?" he almost screamed at me.

A searchlight played across the island from the direction of a powerful engine, closing fast in the darkness. The white British speedboat was back.

A cook in a Bodrum restaurant had tripped, spilling boiling oil over the legs of Irene Maggs, one of our staff, burning her badly. The owner of the boat had volunteered to race her to our doctor, knowing she spoke no Turkish. He had taken the precaution of bringing a Bodrum customs official on board to avoid any later accusations.

Our James Bondian day was over. Irene recovered completely.

Several years earlier Cypriot Ambassador Xenon Rossides had called me from Washington, asking if we would like to undertake excavations in Cyprus. His suggestion was reinforced that summer by an invitation to me from President Kennedy to have luncheon at the White House with his guest of honor, Archbishop Makarios, president of Cyprus.

Although I was involved in our large-scale program in Turkey, we could not let this rare opportunity slip by. I had looked forward to the day when students trained at Yassi Ada would branch off on their own. Michael Katzev was ready. Not only was he familiar with diving and excavation techniques, but he had versed himself thoroughly in the less pleasant details of archaeology, spending winter months helping me prepare budgets, write proposals, choose staff, and order and ship equipment. He had learned foreign antiquities and customs regulations. At the same time, he was an excellent student with a background that included excavation on land.

At the end of summer in 1967, Michael and Susan left Yassi Ada for Cyprus, to conduct an underwater survey. With the guidance of Andreas Cariolou they located the first Classical Greek shipwreck known, near the harbor town of Kyrenia. Michael's ensuing excavation became a model for underwater work in the Mediterranean. He had built on our experiences at Yassi Ada, improving techniques with fresh ideas.

I had been able to provide a compressor and some diving equipment for Michael's survey. I had also promised the *Asherah*, but had to renege. Her assignment in Turkey was only half-fulfilled.

CHAPTER XI

The Search

~~~~~~~~~~~~~~~~~~~~~~~~~~~~~
~~~~~~~~~~~~~~~~~~~~~~~~~~~~~
~~~~~~~~~~~~~~~~~~~~~~~~~~~~~

T<small>HEY</small> looked, somehow, so *American* when they arrived in midsummer 1967: Maurice McGehee, Tony Boegeman, and Bruce Luyendyk, the new sonar team.

It was not that we looked Turkish. After two months on our island kingdom, we had evolved into a new and distinct nationality. Perhaps as defense against the crowded isolation in which we lived, individuality stamped our ethnic costume. Hats seemed important: Claude wore his French army fatigue cap; Susan's straw hat was adorned with an absurd flower, a wire-stemmed plastic tag from the wreck; Yüksel wore a white sailor's cap with brim pulled down all around; I affected a Bodrum sponge diver's cap. Larry molted annually; this summer a white plastic construction helmet, origin unknown, provided his plummage.

Our tribal mores developed unconsciously. If a newcomer brought a hat resembling any already on Yassi Ada, it was greeted with cold stares until abandoned.

Now here were three intruders with American baseball caps.

They stood on the edge of the beach, watching incredulously as our motley group streamed down the side of the island to ladle globs of okra stew onto their plates for lunch. We no longer thought it odd that the cooks lined rolls of toilet paper down the center of our dining table, an infinite supply of napkins. A visiting German doctor had told me that we all suffered a severe case of something which, translated into English, came out as "island fever."

Moving with quiet efficiency, the new arrivals uncrated the sonar equipment they had brought from the Scripps Institution of Oceanography in California. They had come to operate their new sidescanning model, the first of two the navy asked us to evaluate in our survey. Our goals were the wrecks that had yielded the veiled bronze bust, thought by some to represent the goddess Demeter, and the bronze Negro youth. Now in 1967, three years after the *Asherah* was launched, we had found neither wreck, although we had tried.

In 1965 we had spent the summer searching without the *Asherah*, experimenting instead with cheaper, less complex techniques that required a smaller crew and boat. We recalled that underwater television had been used some years earlier to locate a British jet that had crashed into the Mediterranean. For two months we towed a television camera across the seabed in the areas where the bronzes had been netted. We watched the television screen eight hours a day, never turning away, even eating while staring blankly at the monitor in the cabin of the *Mustafa*, a Bodrum trawler.

On board we had as guides Mehmet Imbat, who had found the bronze youth; his uncle, Ahmet Erbin, who had much earlier netted

The bronze bust of a veiled lady pulled from the sea in a sponge dragger's net. Her early identification as Demeter is now disputed.

the so-called "Demeter", and a third captain who had donated to the Bodrum Museum a bronze figurine of the goddess Fortuna, netted in the vicinity of what we now called the Negro Boy Wreck.

Each of the statues had been caught by *kangava,* a Turkish invention used for harvesting sponges. It is basically a four hundred-pound metal axle about twenty-five feet long with metal wheels at either end. As it rolls over the seabed, towed by cable from a boat, it drags a chain to break off sponges that are collected in a following net also attached to the axle.

The sponge captains remembered fairly well where and in what direction they were dragging when they snagged the statues. In order not to waste time by dragging again and again over the same places, they have developed the ability to take shore bearings with a remarkable degree of accuracy by eye, insuring parallel runs. They pull their *kangavas* for several miles at a time before winching them to the surface, however, so they could not pinpoint exactly where any particular object had been caught. They could only show us where they had dragged.

The bronze Negro youth was unrecognizable when first netted (left) but regained his original form when stripped of the covering of concretion.

The "Demeter" had been netted so many years before that we trusted her discoverer's recollection with reservation, deciding to survey a tract of open sea nearly two miles square. In the case of the Negro youth we had a smaller search area: not only had we gone there with Mehmet Imbat only days after he had netted the statue in 1963, but the captain who later netted the Fortuna had pulled his net through the same area at a different angle, providing a cross-reference where the two drag lines intersected. Still we were dealing with a watery expanse perhaps a mile on a side.

When dangling the television camera close enough to the bottom for clear pictures on the screen, we had a field of view only about fifteen feet wide.

"I can take you right across the wreck," Mehmet Imbat said with confidence the first day out. "I've caught amphoras there a dozen times."

He sweated in the sun as he and Oguz Alpözen, the strongest of our archaeology students, lowered and raised hundreds of pounds of TV cable, following directions shouted from the cabin:

"Up, up, up! It's dragging . . . It's too high now. Down a little."

Seaweed and fish were clear on the screen, but we saw no antiquities. Once, when we hauled the cable up at the end of the day, we found a broken amphora handle hanging to the protective cage installed around the camera. We could not guess where it had been hooked.

Mehmet seemed often on the point of tears, more frustrated than we. He thought we didn't believe him, although we assured him of our trust. To approximate the conditions under which he originally worked, we borrowed a *kangava,* removed its chain and net, and buoyed the TV camera about ten feet above its axle, aimed to look forward and slightly down. The method worked beautifully, the accuracy of our search paths apparent from the wheel marks we saw, submarine trails left from our previous passes with the *kangava.*

Several times we entangled the system on underwater rocks. Shefket, the *Mustafa*'s giant captain, then worked alone from his boat's dinghy. Dressed only in his underwear, his face purple, he struggled for hours to free the equipment by giving and taking up slack on hundreds of feet of cable while the rowboat traced on the surface the unraveling movements far below.

Full days were lost when the *meltem* wind rose in the north and

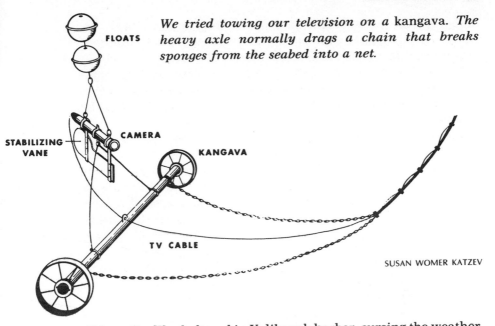

We tried towing our television on a kangava. *The heavy axle normally drags a chain that breaks sponges from the seabed into a net.*

FLOATS

STABILIZING VANE

CAMERA

KANGAVA

TV CABLE

SUSAN WOMER KATZEV

did not die. We sheltered in Yalikavak harbor, cursing the weather, fighting boredom with our own television productions, taking turns as cameramen, actors, and audience. Captain Shefket watched from a harborside coffeehouse the mutiny taking place on his ship. He leapt into his dinghy and rowed with fury toward us, churning the water with his oars, arriving just as Eric, villainous black moustache painted evilly above his lip, threw Larry fully clothed and trussed into the sea from the fantail. Yüksel, electrical engineer Russ Fernald, and I were applauding appreciatively the latest installment of "Perils of Laurence" over the TV set in the cabin.

When the heavy seas did not subside for a week, we sailed southward, to the more protected area where the "Demeter" had been found. We were no more successful. We spotted a few random amphoras, probably Byzantine, and abandoned the effort.

Dr. E.T. Hall, head of the Research Laboratory for Archaeology in Oxford, a center for the development of scientific tools for archaeology, had discovered that slight traces of iron in the clay from which an amphora has been baked are enough, at close range, to affect a proton magnetometer, an instrument used to locate ancient sites by detecting disturbances in the earth's magnetic field caused by iron, or by large walls and pits. He hoped that a large pile of amphoras—a wreck—might be detected from farther away. We tested his instrument without success, although under such poor conditions that our negative results were not conclusive.

Our old friend and sponsor Nixon Griffis arrived later that summer with a Towvane—a towed observation capsule shaped something like the early Mercury space capsules—newly invented by Australian salvager M.E. Lawrie. A man sits in its dry interior, his oxygen supplied from tanks, looking in any direction through a clear plastic window that curves all the way around his head. When towed behind a boat on a thousand or so feet of nylon line, the pilot turns interior wheels that change the angles of a pair of wings, or vanes, on the outside, causing the capsule to plane down through the water. The capsule remains buoyant, staying down only as long as the vanes are depressed at the proper angle and the towing boat provides motion; otherwise it floats to the surface.

The Towvane is far less sophisticated than the *Asherah*, but it had one advantage at that time: it is navigated primarily from the surface, allowing fairly accurate search patterns.

As now almost always happened, I had to return to the university to teach fall classes before the season was over. Larry remained in charge of the survey and told me later he was scared to death. The Towvane had been designed to operate in about 120 feet of water, but the wrecks we sought with it were more than twice that deep,

The Towvane pilot guided his craft close to the bottom. A tender on the boat watched a fathometer to warn him by telephone of unexpected obstacles.

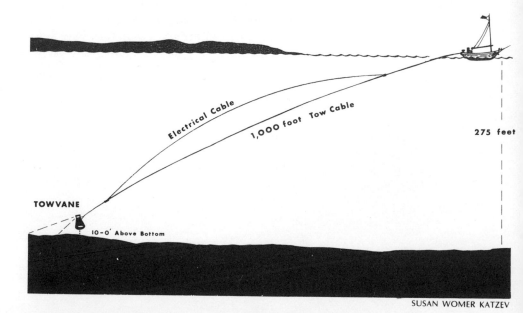

Electrical Cable

1,000 foot Tow Cable

275 feet

TOWVANE

10-0' Above Bottom

presenting a number of unforeseen problems. The vanes weren't large enough to force the capsule to 300 feet against the increasing drag of more and more line in the water. Russ Fernald and fellow engineer Bob Love added extra plywood sheets to the wings to expand their surface area. Eric and Yüksel, taking turns at the controls, next found that it took nearly a mile run to get the Towvane down to the required depth and at least half a mile to turn around, cutting severely into the limited time of the vehicle's life-support system. They also found that the slightest aberration in the angle of one vane, even a centimeter or two, caused the capsule to roll— Yüksel once turned over completely at a depth of nearly 300 feet, bumping his head severely on the inside of the hatch.

Bob and Russ made other improvements needed for depth. They improvised a speaker system that allowed the pilot to give directions directly to the captain of the *Mustafa* without moving his hands from the interior wheels, and added an "angle indicator" to the vane controls, as well as a sort of brake to hold the vanes in place once the critical angle was attained. To mark a potential target they designed a series of marker buoys that were released from the outside of the Towvane by electromagnets.

Eric reported the ride pleasant and easy once down, but "a sort of ground fog over the bottom, starting at about one hundred ninety feet," made search difficult; we had not noticed this layer of suspended silt with the TV, which for some reason cut through it. A fathometer on the *Mustafa* allowed the captain to warn the Towvane pilot of underwater reefs, some of which shot suddenly up from 300 feet to within 100 feet of the surface; still Eric feared crashing into a rock, some of which he just missed at a speed of from four to seven knots, or entangling the towline (an explosive bolt to separate the Towvane from its towing line is part of the original design, but a metalworkers' strike in the United States prevented this from being added if we were to have the capsule at all that summer).

"How did you know if you were retracing your search path?" I asked Eric later in America.

"Oh, easy. I just bumped the bottom every now and then and left a mark on the seabed."

The wrecks were not found. Yüksel was followed and circled by a white shark, one of the few seen during our years in Turkey, but that was all.

At the end of the 1965 survey, our least productive campaign, we were totally discouraged. We had wasted our sponsors' money and our own time. We had simply rediscovered a basic oceanographic principle: the sea is very large.

Then, gradually, we realized the summer had not been a total loss. We had found that the seabed in both search areas was almost completely flat and level. Our failure had been caused by the limited range of visual search; seeing a path only ten to thirty feet wide, we might easily have missed the wrecks by only a few feet. We needed something that could sweep the flat sand for hundreds of feet at a time. Even a long cable might do. Side-scanning sonar seemed a better idea.

Although it has great range—the Scripps unit could search a path 1,200 feet wide—sonar also has limitations. It could tell us that something lay on the ocean floor, but it could tell us little more. We still needed direct observation to determine if that something were an ancient wreck or simply a rocky outcrop on the seabed. We decided we would look for targets with sonar, and inspect each with the *Asherah*.

Which is what brought Maurice, Tony, and Bruce—the Scripps team—to Yassi Ada in 1967.

The drag of increasing amounts of towing line necessitated the enlargement of the capsule's vanes in order to reach a depth of 300 feet.

The sonar "fish," a long, finned unit towed behind and below the *Kardeshler*, transmitted sound waves and received their echoes as they bounced back through the water from the seabed. Any anomaly, either depression or protrusion, showed as a change of tone in the purple lines printed on paper fed from a pair of recorders, for port and starboard, mounted in *Kardeshler*'s hold. Maurice hovered over the recorders, red baseball cap just visible over the top of the open hatch, pipe clenched between his teeth.

Tiny screws and a nut popped from one of the recorders. Although they rested on mattresses, the instruments shook violently from vibration caused by *Kardeshler*'s off-center shaft. The Scripps group found our "research vessel" unbelievable; they were used to oceanographic ships whose operation cost as much per day as we paid for *Kardeshler* and her crew in a month.

Tony and Maurice repaired the damage, completed their sea trials, and said they were ready to go to work.

They sailed south first, to look for the "Demeter" wreck, accompanied by a number of divers from Yassi Ada to assist in navigation from shore-based transit stations.

When they returned, ten days later, they had picked up more than a dozen likely targets. And they had caught some of the enchantment of working the Turkish coast from a lumbering, uncomfortable trawler. Tony and one of *Kardeshler*'s sailors were swapping English and Turkish lessons with impressive results.

The area of the Negro boy wreck was so near Yassi Ada they planned to return to camp each evening.

I accompanied them on their second trip, after strong winds had locked them on the island for days. Don Rosencrantz, who had made most of the arrangements for the search, came too. We scrambled from our beds in almost total darkness, hoping the morning calm would last.

An hour's sail north of Yassi Ada we saw Wreck Rock, a chimney-like island rising straight from the sea like a sentinel guarding the search area. A faint breeze brought fear that the wind might rise, costing another day.

Our transit operators, Larry and two anthropology students, Frank Bartell and Regnar Kearton, were dropped ashore about a mile apart. One at a time they clambered from the dinghy onto the bare rocks where they would swelter in the sun for the rest of the day.

The *Kardeshler* moved out into deeper water and the crew lowered the sonar "fish" over the stern.

A search is a mixture of excitement and boredom. I had learned this in 1965. Eager anticipation rises each morning with the sun, but slowly turns to disappointment with the monotony of passing hours. The routine was unchanging. Every two and a half minutes Tony established radio contact with the three transit operators and began his count down:

"Five. Four. Three. Two. One. *Mark.*"

In the *Kardeshler*'s hold Maurice's poised arms dropped, his thumbs pressing the "mark" buttons on both left and right sonar recorders. A solid line appeared across the paper moving slowly through each. Maurice numbered the lines with green ink.

At the same moment, invisible on the distant shore, the transit operators locked their telescopic sights on the *Kardeshler*'s mast. In turn they radioed their bearings.

The sonar "fish" lowered over the stern of the Kardeshler *during our search for deep shipwrecks.*

The Kardeshler *was designed with her cabin much farther forward than on most Bodrum trawlers, so that she has ample space for survey equipment.*

"This is White One. One eight three degrees." That was Frank.

Larry came in next, "This is White Two. Two three nine degrees," followed by Regnar, or White Three.

Bruce recorded the bearings in his log and calculated our position in the search area. Then he plotted on a chart the exact position of the *Kardeshler* at the moment the "mark" had been made. Directed by the shore transit operators, we could return precisely to any spot where the sonar records had been marked and numbered; if a target appeared between two marks, we could estimate its position by knowing our speed and, therefore, how far we had traveled between the marks made every two and a half minutes.

It was important that no leg of the search pattern be more than six hundred feet from the previous leg, insuring that every square foot of the seabed was scanned twice by the twelve hundred-foot range of the sonar.

My only job was to translate course corrections into Turkish for Captain Mehmet Turguttekin, or his brother Nihat, at the wheel.

Close to shore Maurice called out: "She's shoaling!"

I saw on the sonar paper that the bottom was rising sharply, closing rapidly with the "fish." The normal reaction to avoid collision is to slow down, but Mehmet had been well trained. He gave full throttle to the *Kardeshler,* causing the "fish" to rise in the water as the drag on its cable was increased by our acceleration. At the same time the crew hastily winched in on the cable. The "fish" barely missed the steep underwater hill, passing just over it.

At 2:00 P.M. the *meltem* had begun to blow from the north. Rising waves caused scattered reflections on the sonar records and hundreds of false targets appeared on the paper. We hurried to pick up the transit operators before the sea broke over the rocks where they stood, trapping them against the unscalable cliffs at their backs.

"Another wasted day," I thought, back on Yassi Ada. The Scripps team was already poring over the day's results, two pieces of wrinkled paper two feet wide and fifty feet long. Maurice beckoned me to the workhouse table.

"That's your best target." He pointed to a dark purple speck in the midst of a score of similar specks.

"That's just where the wind came up," I said. "It's like all those other marks around it."

The wind did not die again for days. The sonar team had to return to California for another assignment. They had by then caught a touch of "island fever" themselves; Maurice and Tony told me they hoped to work with us again. They had had only two partial days to perform their electronic wizardry in the area where the Negro youth had been found, an area we had fruitlessly crisscrossed with television for more than a month two years before. Their target was remarkably close to the spot where Mehmet Imbat had then insisted the wreck lay.

The summer drew to a close. Students and teachers returned to universities. We covered the wood of the Roman wreck with sand,

and raised submersible chamber, air lift, tracks, photo tower, water jet, and telephone booth to the surface for winter storage in Bodrum.

Twice during this time the wind dropped for a day, and we made desperate attempts to inspect the sonar target near Wreck Rock with the *Asherah*. Both tries were failures. Once it was so late in the day that Don and Yüksel searched as the sun set, unable to make anything out. The other time they lost their way and came up hundreds of yards from their point of descent.

Martin Klein arrived with another sonar unit, from EG&G International, the second model we were to evaluate. By now I too had to return to teaching, already behind schedule, and left Claude in charge.

As soon as the camp was dismantled, the wind dropped. Larry and Matt Kaplan took up two of the fixed shore stations, setting their transits on bearings that aimed them directly over Maurice's target.

As the *Kardeshler* dropped Larry astern he directed her by radio, correcting her course whenever she began to veer. When she reached Matt's bearing, two miles offshore, she would be directly over the target. Marty Klein's sonar trailed behind and below.

Matt radioed from his post: "You're a hundred yards away . . . now you're fifty yards away . . ."

Don called to Marty. "Watch that recorder. In a few seconds you're going to see the biggest damned target you ever saw."

"Good God! We've really got something big," Marty shouted.

They crossed the target again at right angles, and then again, and again. Each crossing provided additional fixes for the transits. When the sonar showed the *Kardeshler* directly over the target, a buoy was dropped. They towed the *Asherah* from a neighboring cove where she had been anchored earlier in the day.

Yüksel and Don lowered themselves into the submarine from the dinghy. The sound of steel against steel rang across the water as the hatch dropped in place. Claude and Oktay swam out and unhooked the towing bridle. The *Asherah* moved slowly into position by the buoy.

"We have the buoy string in sight," Don radioed. The bubbling sound of flooding ballast tanks melded with the rising whine of twin electric motors as Yüksel threw on full power to force the submarine under.

The antenna for the surface radio was last to disappear. Matt, in the rowboat, holding steady near the buoy, lowered a hydrophone for underwater communications.

"We're at two hundred fifty feet and still can't see bottom . . . we're at two hundred seventy feet . . ." Don relayed a stream of unessential reports to insure the topside crew of the submarine's safe descent.

Suddenly sounds of shouting nearly drowned out crashing and whistling noises over the underwater radio. Was the *Asherah* collapsing?

Only Don and Yüksel were unconcerned. At 285 feet the *Asherah* had reached the bottom of the buoy string. Visibility was limited to only a foot and a half, but the shapes of amphoras—amphoras everywhere—could not be mistaken.

"It's the biggest wreck I've ever seen!" Don shouted, as Yüksel whistled and cheered. Don yelled again into the microphone: "It's a wreck, it's a wreck. We landed right on it." The sound reverberated through the tiny steel sphere surrounding them, mixed with wild banging on a tambourine that Don had, inexplicably, taken on board.

The next day the *Asherah* dived again. The roof tiles of the ancient merchantman's galley lay uncovered, the ship's water storage

Yüksel Eğdemir and Don Rosencrantz, with his submarine tambourine, relax after their dive in the Asherah *to identify the wreck found with sonar.*

A photograph taken from the Asherah *shows amphoras in the cargo of the wreck that yielded the statue of a Negro youth, at a depth of nearly 300 feet.*

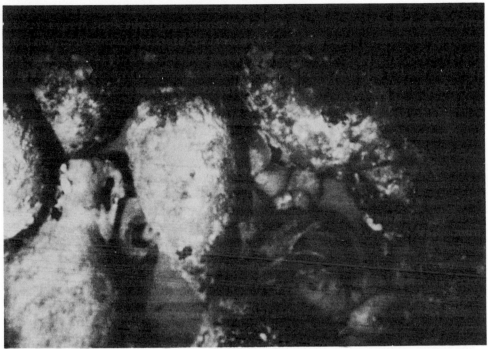

DONALD M. ROSENCRANTZ

jar not far away. Visibility was still too poor to allow mapping with stereophotographs, but Don turned on the exterior lights and snapped a few pictures through a port as Yüksel steered close by the cargo of amphoras.

The expedition ended that day. Most of the team had already overstayed their allotted time. Only packing and shipping remained.

It was the last dive the *Asherah* made for the museum. The insurance premium alone for those few dives had cost as much as a small land excavation. The university had decided we could not operate the submarine without a five-million-dollar liability policy, and we were presented with the bill at the end of the summer. Our program couldn't afford this. We were forced to sell the *Asherah* just as we were beginning to realize her full potential.

The next summer Larry, Frank Bartell, Oktay, and Oguz Alpözen returned to both areas in a small boat with a television system. In the area of the "Demeter" wreck they found that most targets were rocks, but two of the Scripps sonar targets were wrecks—neither probably the wreck that yielded the bust. She had once more eluded us, but the Negro boy wreck was ours. They inspected it again, taking photographs over the TV screen that showed strange shapes in the sand. We await the day when, with mixed-gas equipment, we will be able to dive on the site. Rumor has it that another statue has since been netted in the area and smuggled out of Turkey.

CHAPTER XII
The Chamber

~~~~~~
~~~~~~
~~~~~~

I'VE become superstitious about diving. I wonder if the others have noticed me reaching furtively behind my back to touch wood whenever our safety record is mentioned.

I'd broken my own rule once. I'd been careful, in 1961, never to say aloud what I often thought. But, with only a few weeks remaining in the summer, I bragged in Ankara: "We've proved we don't need professional divers. We haven't come close to an accident." I regretted the words instantly.

Wlady and I drove through the night back to Izmir, then on to Bodrum where we were met by Eric and: "Larry's bent."

The longer I stay with diving, the more worried I become. Every summer is another inning. "Nobody killed. Nobody drowned. Nobody left in a wheelchair." But I don't know how long the game is. When can the announcer say "no-hitter"?

In 1969 we had our most experienced team of divers, our best equipment. We had more than five thousand dives at Yassi Ada behind us, with only Larry's bends to mar a perfect record. Still, more than ever, I stayed on the barge when work was in progress. I found I no longer read between dives, regardless of who was keeping time and who was tending. Perhaps it was because the diving was going so well that I worried.

Larry felt it too.

"I don't like it, George. Everything is going too smoothly. I have nightmares about it."

The wind dropped suddenly in midsummer. Dives were by then routine. Nothing could possibly happen on such a day. I went ashore and, for the first time that summer, relaxed. I was conscious of it as I changed from khaki work clothes into a pair of loud Bermuda shorts and a wildly striped T-shirt brought for party nights. I went to the work house and literally put my feet up to leaf through a book on aerial mapping.

Larry was cleaning an iron concretion behind me. He glanced through the nylon screen at the barge. A diver went over the side, then another. There was no shouting, no commotion—even less running around than he'd often seen from the island. Then the rowboat headed toward the spot above the submersible decompression chamber—to pick up tanks, I thought. Still, something wasn't quite right. Larry stood up and I put my book aside. Everyone on the barge was looking at the boat.

"Something's wrong," Larry said. "Let's go."

He ran out the door and down the side of the island toward the landing with the recompression chamber. Still I held back: "Larry worries *too* much."

Someone called from below. "A diver's injured."

On the way down the steps I could only think that the ballast of the SDC had swung against a diver's head and crushed it. Whoever it was must still be inside the SDC. By now there were a couple of divers snorkeling around it.

Then a black-suited body, tanks still on his back, was thrust up from beneath the water and into the rowboat. As the outboard drew closer I tried to make out who it was. My legs began to shake, slightly.

"It's Eric. He's bent."

"Oh, no. Not *Eric.*" The words were as clear as if I'd said them aloud. I thought of his children, and the fact that Joyce was pregnant.

"Are his pupils dilated?" Dr. David Leith leaned out from the landing as if to reach out and pull the boat still faster toward shore.

Warren Riess pulled back Eric's eyelids. "No."

Eric's body was sprawled askew in the small boat, one arm and his head hanging back over the gunwale. Froth covered his lips, and he made a strangled sucking sound between clenched teeth. It was obvious he was near death.

Hands rushed him to the open door of the chamber. Dave Leith crawled in with him. Door dogged down. Exhaust valves closed. Larry stood with hands up, almost touching the knobs of the control panel. He didn't move. Was he frozen?

"Give him pressure, Larry!" I screamed.

"Not till Dave's got him in the inner chamber. We can't take the whole thing down."

"Dave wants it now. Hurry."

"The air bank won't take the whole chamber to one hundred sixty-five feet."

He was right.

We signaled Dave to pull Eric through the door into the inner chamber and to close the hatch between the two chambers. He was busy working over Eric. He looked up at the window and there was no doubt that he wanted pressure, in a hurry. Eric was threatened with brain death. The difference between 130 and 165 feet of pressure was less important than speed.

Larry opened the main air supply. The sound of rushing air, even outside the chamber, covered all attempts at communication. I

Larry Joline operates the recompression chamber on Yassi Ada during Eric Ryan's treatment for an embolism.

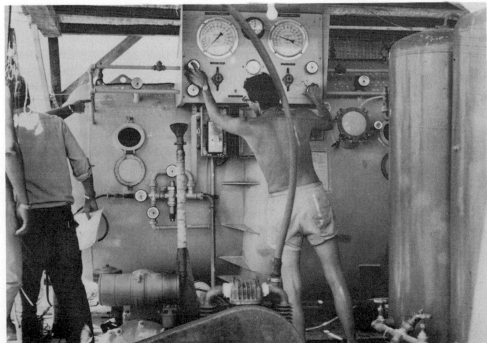

watched the main needle—10 feet . . . 20 feet . . . 30 feet . . . Slowly
. . . 40 feet . . . 50 feet of pressure.

John Owen had started the generator. The chamber lights were
already on. We could see Eric inside. His eyes were open. Dave was
listening to him.

"Jesus, Doc, I really got hit. Let's not do that again!"

The needle passed 80 feet.

"Who's keeping time?" Larry asked.

Sandy Low had the clipboard and treatment tables.

Then 90 feet . . . 100 feet.

All this in a matter of minutes. Chief Diver Bob Henry had helped
Eric from the boat and was still standing next to me, dripping wet.
He had been with Eric on the dive. He hadn't decompressed.

"Go on back to the SDC and just stay there for a good long time.
What if you get bent?"

The needle rose more and more slowly. At 130 feet it stopped. The
air bank was empty. The compressor was running, but it would take
time to build the bank up again.

We explained to Dave what the problem was and he moved with
Eric into the inner chamber. He didn't need 165 feet of pressure
anyway. He'd treat Eric on the latest oxygen tables. Back they went
to 60 feet. Eric put on an oxygen mask.

Now it was a matter of waiting. Of keeping time. Of ventilating
the chamber. Of preparing the barge compressor as a back-up for
the chamber. Of bringing spare tanks in from the barge. Barbara
Leith was timekeeper and stuck by her post on the barge until all
the divers were out of the water. She followed what was happening
by radio. As we waited we pieced together what had taken place.

Eric and Bob Henry had followed the white cord from the telephone booth up the slope to the SDC, about fifty yards away. There
they were to decompress for eight minutes on a large steel ring
hanging just ten feet below the open bottom hatch of the SDC before
swimming up into the chamber above. Bob noticed Eric pounding
on his knee, trying to signal something, and reached over to help
him rub it. Then he saw a handful of shells Eric had collected
falling slowly from his hand. Eric's eyes were looking ahead but not
seeming to see. Water had started rising in his mask.

Don Callender had just finished decompressing, and as he left the
SDC he swam down and gave Eric a friendly punch on the shoulder.

He was surprised that there was no response. Bob signaled Don back up into the chamber, ripped Eric's clenched hands from the steel ring, and shoved his now rigid body through the hatch. He was about to stop breathing. They forced air into him from his own regulator, but when he lost the mouthpiece and his teeth clenched up they turned to mouth-to-mouth resuscitation.

Eric later remembered the water rising in his mask. "I knew I was drowning, but I just couldn't do anything about it." And he thought he remembered Bob Henry's voice saying, on the SDC telephone to the island, "We have an emergency here."

We watched Eric through the thick glass port of the larger room in the chamber. He gave the diver's sign for O.K. and a smile. Dave made continuous notes as he checked reflexes and made examinations I didn't understand. We sent food and water through the lock.

The pressure gradually was lowered. Hours later we stood in a receptive semicircle as the door opened and Eric stepped out unsupported. He had dried blood under his nose, and looked exhausted, but he was fit. Cameras snapped. We shook hands all around. And then, with little assistance, Eric went up the concrete steps from the landing to the higher part of the island, and then along the path to Claude's old "slum" house, which he was sharing.

Eric Ryan is greeted by Claude Duthuit as he climbs unassisted from the chamber into which he was carried, near death, only hours before.

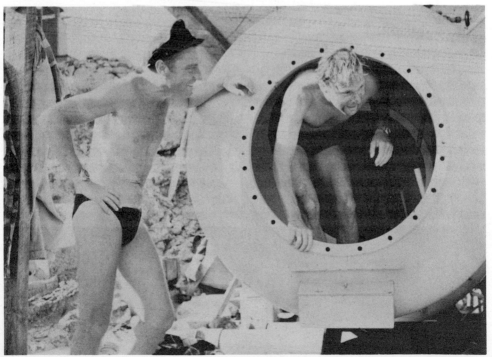

ELLEN HERSCHER

We were all radiantly happy. I brought Dave, Bob, Larry, Sandy Low, and John Owen to my tent for a well-deserved drink. Dave warned us that Eric would probably suffer a relapse because of swelling around the spot where the bubble had damaged his spine or brain. But just to have Eric alive was a joy.

We took turns visiting him, squeezing into Claude's little hut. At one point I noted that I was looking at Eric and Claude and Larry and Yüksel, just those four, and I was reminded of a picture in the *National Geographic* of the same four—Eric, Claude, and Yüksel were holding Larry that time as he collapsed from an embolism or the bends.

Eric's relapse came faster than I had expected. He had walked almost normally from the chamber, but soon he could only get across the hut with difficulty, his legs losing sensation and becoming weaker by the hour. Fred, Peter Fries, Larry, Claude, and John Owen were to take shifts sitting up with him through the night, but all of us stayed together talking to Eric. He was afraid to leave his legs still for long, or to go to sleep; he could barely urinate. We laughed at him as he staggered across the floor, stumbling without a hand to help him. We kidded him unmercifully, and he laughed back with us. But he was worried. If we distracted him from his worsening condition for only a few minutes at a time perhaps it was worth it. Dave made periodic visits.

When the sun finally came up, I went to the various manuals and papers, including the latest navy treatment tables, on embolism. I read each again and again. Dave was the doctor and I trusted his judgment completely, but I wanted to be sure we had tried everything. I met Dave on the island path in the cold morning air. We both felt that further recompression could not help Eric—he had breathed oxygen under pressure for so long there couldn't still be a bubble causing the trouble—but it couldn't hurt. We decided to try once more, and Eric was game.

Dave had spent so much time in the chamber already that I asked if I could go in with Eric this time. The team outside was ready again, but Bob Henry operated the valves since he had at least had a little sleep. The chamber grew warmer as compressed air rushed in. Eric kept trying his leg. There was no change. Just before we opened the hatch at the end of the treatment I scribbled a hasty note and held it to the window behind my back: "No pictures this time." Nor were there handshakes.

Oğuz took one of the boats to Karatoprak to call a taxi from Bo-drum to take Eric to the hospital in Izmir. Drained, we walked around the island, pecking at breakfast, deciding who would go to Izmir with him. Eric sat outside the hut shaving, the most cheerful person in camp. Smiles and jokes were forced now. I went in and watched Claude packing Eric's bag; it was hard to go back outside. I walked quickly away, to be alone, but I met Larry on the path.

"Oh, Larry, we love him so much."

Larry put his arms around my shoulders and said, "Go ahead, George. Have a good cry. Ann and I just did."

As Eric sailed off for Karatoprak with Claude and Dave Leith we gave the shout that Eric knew was coming:

"Bye bye, stupid."

I visited him in the air force hospital, where a neurologist re-ported an air bubble had been trapped at the base of Eric's skull, cutting off much of the circulation to his brain. An embolism—and there was now little doubt that it was this he suffered, rather than a normal case of bends—is often caused by a panicky diver rising rapidly without exhaling. This was impossible in Eric's case; we still do not know what caused his accident.

Eric forced himself out of bed and hauled himself around the room, stumbling, rejecting proffered aid as if pride alone would enable him to walk again. Old friends came through to cheer him with stories of their own diving accidents and how they had recov-ered. Larry recounted a similar weakness during his own recupera-tion. Mustafa Kapkin dropped in and told about his case of bends, from which he had recovered. Wlady was in Turkey on a short visit when he learned of Eric's accident; he had been diving profession-ally in California the year before, when he was totally paralyzed on one side and recovered only because a helicopter was able to rush him to a nearby chamber. *National Geographic* photographer Bates Littlehales came by and told how he'd been cured of bends from an archaeological dive in Mexico.

When he could walk with the aid of a cane, Eric moved first to a hotel, then back to Yassi Ada to exercise his legs before returning home. He never regained complete sensation in his left leg.

Ironically, the embolism had struck in the middle of our most pleasant and productive summer on Yassi Ada. With proven techniques and mostly experienced excavators, work was smooth and efficient. We found the galley of the Roman ship, with a full assortment of lamps, plates, cooking wares, and other objects, which dated it to the end of the fourth century A.D. The port half of the ship's hull was extraordinarily well preserved. At the end of the campaign we had all but completed its excavation in the 1,200 man hours I had predicted we could achieve in only two seasons with our new methods.

After Eric's accident we tightened our already stringent safety practices. We abandoned the SDC altogether so that divers were never far from the barge where our doctor was stationed. We quit using the outboard to ferry staff and visitors between the barge and Yassi Ada, keeping it tied always to the barge for a quick trip to the chamber on the island. We repeatedly rehearsed each person's duty in case of an emergency, and had several back-ups for each position to take a potential victim's place on the roster. And we bought a silver policeman's whistle in Bodrum. It would be blown only in case of dire emergency.

The whistle's eerie sound wakened me one night, raising the hair on my neck. The entire camp was up at once, racing for appointed

We met in the workhouse on Yassi Ada after breakfast and lunch each day to plan upcoming dives and assign specific tasks.

posts at the chamber, barge, and generators. A young Bodrum diver, one leg paralyzed, had been brought to us. His treatment was efficient and successful. We were pleased with ourselves.

The summer drew to a close. When there were only seven divers left, Bob Henry and Dr. John Miller—Dave Leith's replacement during the last month—went down to cover the wreck again with sand.

From the barge I saw a small, green sponge boat approach. I assumed it was heading for the reef, where I had seen it several days before. But it was coming straight for the barge.

"It's bends," I said to Yüksel.

My intuition was correct. We saw a large man lying on the foredeck, his legs drawn up, rolling from side to side in pain.

I hammered the pipe hanging into the water from the barge. Bob Henry's voice, high pitched from pressure, answered from the phone booth:

"What's up?"

"We've got a bent sponge diver here."

"What kind of decompression do we have?"

"Come on up now. We'll send word down to the stop."

I wrote figures on the message board and dropped it over the side to the first decompression stop; at the same time I sent the sponge boat on toward the chamber, assuring the divers a doctor was on his way.

When we reached the island, the fat man lay on the concrete platform. His skin was a grey I had not seen before. His eyes were closed. With Yüksel translating, he complained of terrible stomach pains. His companions said that he had dived to nearly one hundred feet for an hour and a half before coming directly to the surface without decompressing.

Several of the crew moved him into the outer room of the chamber, where he was joined by John Miller, still dripping in his wetsuit pants.

At sixty feet of pressure the stricken diver showed no improvement. John decided to go to a treatment table requiring 165 feet of pressure. They were still in the outer lock, the door to the inner lock open.

John Miller, on the telephone: "I can't get him into the inner lock. He's too heavy."

"Mehmet," Yüksel called into the telephone speaker—and we now knew the diver's name for the first time—"Mehmet, try to get into the next room. Try to help the doctor."

John Owen at the window saw no movement. Then: "He's pushing with his legs. He's trying to help." At last they were inside. Bob sent the chamber to 165 feet.

The result was not good. Mehmet's condition still worsened. They went back to sixty feet and pure oxygen.

Mehmet could talk now. John Miller asked us to lock Yüksel into the chamber to translate. There was something wrong: the bends in Mehmet's arm was responding to treatment, but his stomach was worse. He spit up blood. John suspected something more than the bends, and asked Yüksel to learn if the man had a history of stomach troubles. Yes, he had had a chronic peptic ulcer for seventeen years.

We learned more about Mehmet. He had five children, most of them grown. He was not a sponger, as we had thought, but a barber. He didn't need to dive to make a living. He was doing it just for fun.

Yüksel, out of the chamber, motioned me to the little sponge boat tied up at the landing. It was getting dark. A small kerosene lamp flickered through a dusty pane of glass.

"Look how they live," he said. "Look at that. That's all they got in a day." He pointed to a pathetic pile of uncleaned sponges on the deck.

"What's it worth?" I asked.

"Thirty or forty liras." Maybe three dollars.

A half-moon ran in and out among the clouds as we ate dinner around the chamber, taking turns at the controls. When I watched at the chamber window, I saw John feverishly inspecting his patient. The compressor was running to refill.the air bank for ventilation, and communications were poor. John held a note to the window saying something about a burst ulcer.

I wrote back, "Is that very bad?"

"Yes, he seems to be developing perotonitis. Bring me a vial of chloromycetin, a five cc. syringe, and water for injection."

When we locked the medicine into the chamber, Mehmet was already in critical condition. It was now a matter of getting him to surgery as fast as possible. Otherwise, John said, he would die. It was the first time I had heard death mentioned around the chamber. I asked Bob how soon they could come back to surface pressure.

"They're committed to the table and will have to ride it out." He nonetheless began calculations to see if they could come out sooner.

Mehmet vomited and could no longer keep an oxygen mask on. Yüksel was called to the loudspeaker from time to time to translate instructions to him. Once John Miller called for a translation of something Mehmet was saying. The Turks among us stood looking out to sea. They didn't need headphones to hear the cries, which even I could understand. Mehmet was no longer describing his pain or condition. He was calling to Allah. John gave him a shot of morphine. I was sitting on the edge of the concrete landing when John Owen brought word that John Miller wanted Yüksel and me in the chamber for a conference. I don't know if I asked the question or only looked questioningly at him:

"He died."

Yüksel and I sat quietly in the outer lock as the air rushed in, sending us to the same pressure as John Miller. When the pressure was equal, we opened the door between the two rooms.

"I'm sorry, George. He convulsed and died. I resuscitated him and he took a couple of breaths, and then he convulsed and his heart stopped. There was no point in trying to revive him again." Then, to Yüksel: "Have his friends been told?"

"I don't know. But they feel it happened."

We left John behind to complete his decompression. For the first time I realized the loneliness of a doctor fighting to save a man's life. It was the first time he had had a patient die in a chamber, John said. John Owen offered to replace Yüksel and me in the chamber, to keep him company as he sat crowded against the dead man.

I stepped out first and looked at the ground; Yüksel followed. *"Başiniz sağ olsun,"* he said simply, "Long may you live."

Two hours later it was over. We opened the chamber, strapped Mehmet's body to a wooden stretcher and placed it on one of our boats for the sail back to his village.

Next morning was the greyest I had yet seen at Yassi Ada. The sea resembled the Atlantic on an overcast day, totally unlike the Aegean we had dived in for ten years.

The steady throb of a one-cylinder engine came from around the island as we ate breakfast. It was a sound we now feared, but this was the same sponge boat coming back to take us to an inquest. I put on the cleanest clothes I had on the island and joined Yüksel and John Miller. Yüksel advised me to accept the previous day's sponges offered to us by the crew as repayment for trying to help their friend.

We sailed up the coast to Gümüşlük, about half an hour away, and into the small but well-sheltered bay where ten years earlier I had snorkeled over the harbor walls of ancient Myndus. The harbor today holds a single pier, a rickety patchwork of stray bits of wood nailed to uprights driven into the sand. It is a poor village.

The old men in the waterfront teahouse called the usual greeting: *"Hoş geldiniz. Welcome."*

"Hoş bulduk," we answered, and shook hands.

Someone brought tea; we offered condolences as we drank. The inquest was at a house about fifteen minutes away by foot.

Rounding a bend in the dusty road we came upon a huge crowd of women wearing identical black-and-white striped shawls around their heads. This was Mehmet's house. At the next house the men stood together. In all there were at least a hundred people. Under the shade of branches over a little patio sat the Bodrum judge, the official government doctor, the commander of the Bodrum gendarmerie, and a clerk with typewriter. The judge had visited Yassi Ada only a few weeks earlier, and we had discussed the responsibilities of treating divers who were not members of our own group; we were, of course, not licensed to treat patients in Turkey. We had been advised to do the humane thing. John now described the case as statements were written and signed by officials. Someone apologized that we had been brought away from our work. There would be no autopsy, though John had hoped for one, because there was no legal reason for it. While statements were being prepared, two men passed with a wooden carrier of flat boards, a headpiece nailed to one end. The muezzin climbed onto the roof of the dead man's house and, as the typewriter continued, began his wailing chant, hands cupped to his mouth.

The widow appeared, supported on each side by an older woman, crying and tossing her head violently; she ripped the shawl from her head and threw it to the ground, flailing her arms and striking her body in frustration. She seemed surprisingly young and attractive.

Our duties over, we turned to leave. The widow lay on the ground in the midst of a small group of women, still purging herself of grief. Later we learned that Mehmet was popular in the village and had no enemies.

CHAPTER XIII
AINA

~~~~~~~~~~~~~~~~~~~~~~~~~~~~~~~~~~~~
~~~~~~~~~~~~~~~~~~~~~~~~~~~~~~~~~~~~
~~~~~~~~~~~~~~~~~~~~~~~~~~~~~~~~~~~~

BY 1967 I was directing the largest diving project in the world. I hadn't realized it until a professional diver pointed it out. I checked with the navy and found that it was true.

No one else—not navy teams, oil drillers, salvage firms, nor oceanographic institutes—had twenty-five divers working twice a day at one hundred forty feet, six days a week, for months at a time. By 1969 we had made more than eight thousand decompression dives, experimented with one of the first research submarines launched, conducted a search program with sonar and underwater television, and designed and built new types of diving and underwater mapping equipment.

Even smaller operations were run by large, permanent staffs. I was trying to do it alone. Not even that. I was doing it in my spare time. I was teaching as much as other professors at the university, reading as many term papers, advising on as many doctoral theses. During most of the time I had no access to a departmental secretary, and usually typed my own correspondence.

At the end of the 1969 season I went directly from Yassi Ada to England, to spend a sabbatical year as a visiting scholar at St. John's College, Cambridge. The museum hired David Owen for two years, to take my place while I was away and to assist me on my return; it was then that he organized and directed the excavation of a fifth-century B.C. wreck in the Straits of Messina.

When I returned to Philadelphia the following fall, after a productive year in England, I had made the decision to leave underwater archaeology. The accidents at Yassi Ada in 1969 probably influenced me, but mainly I did not want to return to the life that I had led. Something was bound to suffer: the safety of the diving program, the timely publication of archaeological results, or the quality of the courses I taught at the university. Further, with a growing family I was no longer willing to return to the museum every night and work until the small hours of the morning to get the job done.

I had directed the museum's underwater program for a decade, perhaps long enough. Most of our success had been due to youth and naïveté. We had been too ignorant to know why things couldn't be done. Few members of the diving community had believed in 1960 that a group of archaeologists could learn to dive well enough to conduct major underwater operations on their own, but we had ignored their pessimism. Had I known more prehistory when I went to Cape Gelidonya I might not have found evidence of Semitic seafaring there; I would have *known* it could not exist in the Bronze

After removing several ribs, Fred van Doorninck marks the ends of treenails (wooden pegs) with white thumbtacks, to aid in mapping the Roman hull.

MUSTAFA KAPKIN

Age Aegean. If I had understood the technical reasons given by professional photogrammetrists for the impossibility of using aerial survey techniques under water, I would not have tried them. I might have taken the advice of a senior officer in the successful search for the submarine *Thresher,* who told me in 1967 that we could not expect to find ancient wrecks with side-scanning sonar and should not waste our time. Time and again we had ignored expert opinion—"It just won't work"—finding simple solutions to problems said to be too complex for us to understand. Now I was an "expert." Too often I found myself brushing off suggestions from new students with a brusque "it won't work."

Dr. Rainey knew my feelings. At a cocktail party he mentioned that one of my former students, Peter Vinson, then teaching at the University of California, had discovered a promising Neolithic and Bronze Age site on land in southern Italy. The museum would sponsor its excavation if I would direct it in 1971.

A few days after my arrival in Italy we began digging. We had rented the field in which the prehistoric settlement lay and surveyed it, hired workmen, and found housing in nearby Gravina di Puglia. Shovels, wheelbarrows, and surveying and drafting equipment were all obtained locally. We had not needed a month of preparations on the site; there were not twenty-odd machines to keep in running order; I did not worry about the safety of the students; and I had had to do no fund raising during the preceding winter.

The site was rich. Peter Vinson and I found new evidence for the arrival of the first domestic animals in the region. Yet, as I troweled through habitation debris, the thought recurred: If these animals were introduced from the East, from the coasts of Greece or Yugoslavia, one of the ships that carried them must lie on the bottom of the Adriatic. That ship, properly excavated, might answer more questions about immigration and new influences than a dozen similar land sites.

I drove occasionally to the port towns of Bari and Brindisi to meet arrivals by air and sea. The sound of diesel engines and the smell of tar transported me to Bodrum. I did not have that much to offer at Gravina. I had not dug a similar site on land before, without walls and obvious architectural remains. I was learning often from my students, some with considerable experience. Was I not wasting my experience at sea?

A camera specially designed for our stereo mapping in 1969 gave excellent results. The camera housing had a special lens for undistorted underwater pictures, and the shutter was triggered electrically to avoid any camera movement. Bob Henry uses it.

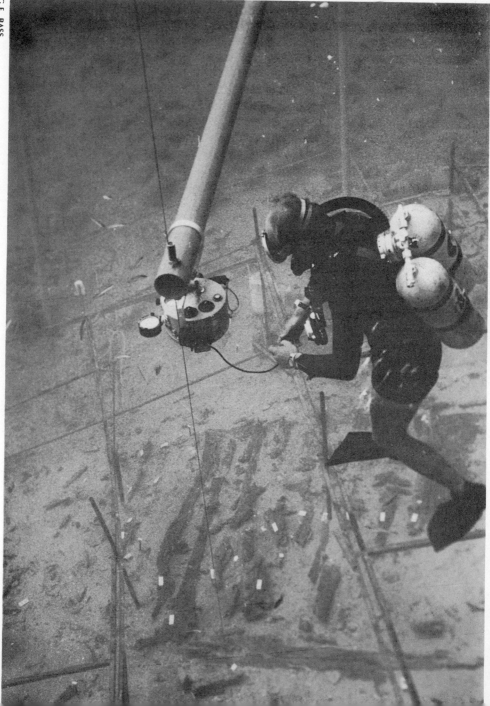

G.F. BASS

I gave a talk on the excavation that fall at the University Museum. The slides were good. The results exciting. But something was lacking.

"You just don't have your heart in this, George," Ann said afterward.

I realized I had made a mistake. Rather than leave underwater archaeology because of the problems, why not try to overcome the problems? If I never came up with another fresh idea, at least I had the experience to raise funds and organize the work. The idea of a permanent center or institute of nautical archaeology began to jell, an institute with its own research vessel, its own crew, its own permanent staff of archaeologists and engineers, with conservator, artist, photographer, and other specialists.

I talked daily about it with David Owen. I drove to Colgate, where Eric and I discussed it at length. We would search for shipwrecks in the Mediterranean, trace early trade routes into the Black Sea, follow Classical sailing directions for the Red Sea, and sail out through the Straits of Gibralter in the wake of the earliest explorers. We pictured a floating archaeological center, fully equipped for electronic surveys, saturation diving, submarine support, and full-scale excavations, with conservation laboratory, machine shop, library, darkroom, drafting room, and classrooms on board. Perhaps a large, steel-hulled catamaran with ample deck space would do.

I was still concerned about the responsibilities of a diving operation.

"Was it worth it, Eric?" I asked, referring to the remaining numbness from the embolism.

"Hell, yes, it was worth it. You don't know how long you'll live. I try to make every day an adventure in some way."

Since we had known him, Eric had broken one leg skiing and another sky diving, had found himself in the middle of a gun battle during a visit to Vietnam, and had suffered an embolism while diving. But his enthusiasm for life did not revolve around physical danger. He remained, primarily, an artist.

"Look at that, George," he exclaimed during a Colgate football game. "Yeah," I answered, keeping my eyes on the running play. Eric was not watching the field. He was looking away at the golds and reds that emblazoned the autumn hills of upper New York state.

He would not be able to dive with us, but somehow, I knew, he would be with us in the Mediterranean again.

"Let me know when you get that catamaran," he called after me as I pulled out of his driveway.

A month later, just after Christmas, Eric was dead of pneumonia. An autopsy showed no signs of the embolism having contributed to his death. I remember him best staring at the crimson hills above the football stadium. He was just 41.

In March 1972 I met with the board of managers of the University Museum and read a statement proposing the establishment of a center or institute devoted entirely to marine archaeology, to be part of the museum. Our program would include spring seminars on the history of seafaring, summer excavations, autumn surveys, and winters devoted to publishing and preparing for the following year. The annual budget would be a minimum of $100,000, but I pointed out I did not intend to ask the museum to finance it; I would try to raise the necessary funds, even for my own salary. The museum had nothing to lose, and possibly a unique center to gain. The board voted enthusiastically to accept the principle of the institute.

Months passed, but little more happened. Differences of opinion over the proposed institute's structure remained unresolved. The director of the institute, I felt, could not be a faculty member, but should hold a nonteaching post similar to that of the head of the museum's applied science center; the museum said this would not be possible, even if I found the required salary. I felt we had a duty to conserve the wrecks we would excavate, but this was against museum policy; Michael Katzev, after excavating the Kyrenia wreck for the museum, was restoring it under Oberlin College auspices. Neither the museum nor I felt we could compromise such basic differences. With no hard feelings, I realized that the formation of the institute as part of the museum would solve none of the unique problems of underwater archaeology that we had faced in the past. A separate institute seemed the only solution.

I decided to resign from the University of Pennsylvania, giving a year's notice in September so that a replacement could be found. Colleagues advised me to ask for a year's leave of absence—to see if I could form the institute or not—or at least not to announce my resignation until spring. I felt that either move would have been unfair to the museum to which I still felt great loyalty. I wrote to Dr. Young with my resignation. He suggested I had the "forty fidgets," but did not try to dissuade me.

I felt suddenly very much alone. I had abandoned the security of a tenured professorship with the many benefits a university offers. If I could not succeed in putting the institute together by June, I would be looking for some other line of work.

I quickly learned that none of the major foundations, which had supported our past work, was willing to support the same work under the aegis of a new institute.

I wrote my news to Jack Kelley, a businessman and avid diver, in Tulsa; he had earlier discussed possible financial support of our research. Jack called immediately after receiving the letter, offering a three-year pledge of funds to the proposed institute, and agreeing to serve on its board of directors.

Steven Gadon, our family lawyer, volunteered enthusiastically to help us incorporate and obtain the proper status as a scientific/educational organization, which could receive tax-deductible gifts like any university or museum.

"What shall we call the organization?" he asked.

I thought for a moment: "The American Institute of Nautical Archaeology."

An institute cannot be a single man. We needed staff to assure continuity. Michael Katzev had moved to Cyprus to oversee the restoration of the Kyrenia ship. He and Susan were excited by the prospects and agreed to serve on AINA's staff.

John Gifford, who had worked with us at Yassi Ada in 1969, was finishing work on an M.S. in marine sciences at the University of Miami. Since 1969 he had headed his own archaeological project in the Bahamas, and had been chief scientist in an underwater habitat operation. He was eager to join us.

Fred van Doorninck, David Owen, and Joseph Shaw (an authority on ancient harbors) agreed to serve as adjunct professors of the institute; they would retain their present teaching posts, but might join us for summer courses and excavations, and would also be able to head their own projects under AINA auspices.

Jack Kelley told me that his friend, John Baird, would match his pledge and would also serve on the board of directors; Bill Searle, who had helped me so much when he was chief of navy diving, had already agreed to sit on the board, along with Melvin Payne, president of the National Geographic Society.

During the months prior to our first board meeting I was convinced I had contracted a terrible and incurable disease. I could not sleep through a night. Doctors, for enormous fees, couldn't find anything wrong, but suggested that it was nerves.

The morning of the meeting I waited anxiously with Steve Gadon in a conference room of the Benjamin Franklin Hotel in Philadelphia. I wondered how many people would attend.

At 10:00 A.M. John Brown Cook of the Cook Foundation, which had given substantial support to Michael's Kyrenia project, entered; his foundation had already pledged money to AINA for five years. Nixon Griffis, our initial sponsor for the Cape Gelidonya excavation, followed. Jack Kelley and John Baird and Bill Searle arrived, as did Harry Kahn, a Philadelphia businessman and diver. Betsy Whitehead, secretary of the Archaeological Institute of America, announced a personal three-year pledge, and Melvin Payne came with a check for $15,000 from the National Geographic Society, to support our first field project.

G. Kenneth Sams, W. Willson Cummer, and Fletcher Blanchard, professors of classics, architecture, and engineering respectively, represented the purely academic side of the board; all had worked with me at Yassi Ada and understood the problems of underwater archaeology. They were joined by Alan Boegehold, chairman of the Classics Department at Brown University. Brown, Bryn Mawr College, and the universities of North Carolina, Cincinnati, New Hampshire, and California at Berkeley had agreed to be annual supporting institutes of AINA, and Alan volunteered to try to increase their number.

I was elected president, Michael vice-president, and Steve Gadon secretary/treasurer, with Ann as assistant treasurer. Michael, John Gifford, Ann, and I would live in the Mediterranean to be near the work. To handle and coordinate institute affairs in the United States, Cynthia Jones Eiseman was appointed executive director. Cynthia, who had worked with me at Yassi Ada, was writing her doctoral thesis at the University of Pennsylvania on the fifth-century B.C. shipwreck she had helped David Owen excavate in Italy.

Ann and I sold our house and most of our possessions. With only eight crates of archaeological books and her grand piano, we sailed in June 1973, with our sons Gordon and Alan, for Cyprus, where we would settle at least temporarily near the Katzevs, who already had bought a house there.

We had a new archaeological institute. We did not have a site to excavate. Our first task was to find one. Michael, David Owen, and

I had excavated wrecks of the thirteenth, fifth, and fourth centuries B.C., and the fourth and seventh centuries A.D. I hoped we might find at least one wreck that would fill the chronological gaps between them.

With the grant from the National Geographic Society, and sonar and diving equipment loaned to us by the University Museum, I went to Turkey with John Gifford. Our survey team also included John Broadwater, electrical engineer; Donald Frey, a physics professor who had headed an earlier sonar survey for me in Turkey and dived at Yassi Ada; Donald Rosencrantz, now working for the Naval Undersea Center in Hawaii; and Joseph Alexander, a new volunteer.

Fred is assisted by Peter Fries in making careful measurements and drawings of a rib from the Roman wreck.

CHAPTER XIV
Luck

$$\rightsquigarrow\rightsquigarrow\rightsquigarrow\rightsquigarrow\rightsquigarrow$$

JOE Alexander stretched and rolled onto his stomach, basting in his own sweat. Buoys—numbered orange cans tied by various lengths of string to melon-sized rocks—surrounded him. He lay on a wooden platform projecting from the stern of *Günyel,* our thirty-five-foot Turkish fishing boat.

In *Günyel's* enclosed cabin John Broadwater watched the sonar recorder through eyes bleared by diesel fumes. His face had a greenish pallor and his moustache seemed to droop lower over the corners of his mouth.

"What about that one?" I asked, squinting at the recorder from the cabin hatch. I could just distinguish a purple smudge appearing on the damp sonar paper.

"I don't know," John's Kentucky drawl slowed his answer, "it might be something."

I turned to Joe:

"Starboard buoy!"

Joe raised himself. "How deep?"

"How deep is it, John?"

"About one hundred eighty feet," he answered.

"One hundred eighty feet," I relayed.

Joe chose a buoy with two hundred feet of string.

"Hell, we've missed it by now. Let's go back and try to pick it up again."

John looked up at me. "I really don't think it's anything," he said without expression.

We swept in a wide arc, the sonar "fish" trailing behind us. We did not see the target again. I don't think any of us expected to.

Throughout August and September 1973, we had searched for wrecks below the steep cliffs between Bodrum and Antalya, bracketing sonar targets with buoys, then identifying them with underwater television—a tedious routine that often consumed half a day for a single target. Whole days passed without a likely mark on the sonar paper, and all the targets but one had proved to be simply rocks jutting from the seabed.

The exception, in a bay just northeast of Bodrum, lay in water more the color of a muddy South Carolina river than transparent Aegean blue. We videotaped a few possible fragments of pottery as Captain Mehmet patiently dangled the TV camera inches above the bottom, taking care not to stir up more silt. But even using "stop action" in playing the tape, we were not sure what we had found.

Joe, Yüksel, and Don Frey volunteered to examine the site, only

John Broadwater studies a sonar record as it emerges from our recorder. Objects protruding from the seabed appear as dark shadows on the paper.

seventy feet deep. We hadn't planned to dive before the arrival of AINA's new double-lock chamber, but the freighter bringing it from America was behind schedule and the big Yassi Ada chamber was far too large for any local boat.

"You can't see anything," Don reported as he returned from the thick sepia liquid. "We held hands to stay together."

"Do you know how I found the bottom?" Yüksel added. "I sank into it up to my shoulder before I knew I had reached it."

On a later dive John Broadwater blindly grappled a handful of shards, probably Late Roman or Byzantine. Does the deep mud conceal an ancient hull in near perfect condition? We still don't know.

Each of us covered his disappointment in a different way. Our engineers modified equipment, wrestled with batteries, and made repairs. At least they stayed busy. But Joe had come to Turkey to dive, and found himself instead sitting for weeks on a rough wooden perch built out over the water. With exaggerated motions he "practiced" his technique of throwing buoys, bragging of the skill it required:

"I don't know how you could replace me, George."

His infectious grin, an even white streak in a tanned face, masked frustration.

When our new chamber finally reached Izmir we transferred from *Günyel* to the larger *Kardeshler*. Mehmet let me have her as cheaply as possible, but the trawler's large, permanent crew required salaries whether looking for fish or ancient wrecks. The fair price represented a fortune from our dwindling funds.

We watched more money slip away as the *Kardeshler,* already stripped of fishing gear to make room for diving equipment, lay idle for a week in Bodrum harbor. The new chamber's patient-to-tender telephone was listed as a "radio" on its shipping documents. We had permission to import a chamber but not a radio, and we could not convince Izmir customs officials that it was, in fact, not a radio but an integral part of the chamber. We offered to rip it out. The officials wanted to help, but their rules were clear.

While an inspection of the "radio" by a professor of electronics at a nearby technical college was scheduled, we returned to the *Günyel* for a hectic, sleepless wild-goose chase after a wreck reported seventy miles away, losing a day trapped in a harbor by high winds and most of another lost in a fog. By the time the telephone had been identified, and the chamber mounted with compressors and air bank on *Kardeshler*'s deck, Joe, Don Frey, and Don Rosencrantz had returned to America. We were down to three divers.

To replenish the staff, I hired Merih Karabag, the mechanically inclined young landlord of our rented Bodrum rooms, and Cumhur Ilik. Cumhur (pronounced Jumhur) had been a ship's boy at Cape Gelidonya thirteen years before, but I had seldom seen him afterward. He had since become a sponge diver, retired from that, and now operated his own charter boat out of Bodrum. He was free to join us only because the tourist season was over.

It was not only a shrinking staff that needed augmenting; we had spent most of the $15,000 National Geographic grant. I was not sure where to turn for additional funds. Although the future of AINA depended on the outcome of the survey, I was hesitant to appeal to its board so soon for help since we had almost nothing to show for our efforts so far. They might well wonder if they had backed the wrong horse.

I knew one man, Dr. Leonard Carmichael, chairman of the Committee for Research and Exploration at the National Geographic Society, to whom I could turn with little embarrassment. He had followed my work from its beginnings, sitting on the boards of several foundations and societies that had supported it. He had seen us succeed each year. He knew we were a good risk. I wrote to him asking for a supplemental grant of $2,000, promising that shortly we would locate good wrecks; now that we could dive, we would follow leads from local divers. We then weighed anchor and sailed for Bozburun, a sponging village far down the coast.

Bozburun appears two-dimensional from the sea, a movie set of white and yellowing rectangular facades, red-tiled roofs scarcely varying in height below a backdrop of brown, barren hills. Mehmet rowed ashore with his sailors looking like a pirate landing party in wool knit caps. He returned to say he had found a sponge diver willing to show us wrecks.

I followed him back with Yüksel and joined *Kardeshler*'s crew outside the harbor coffeehouse, where we slowly sipped cups of thick, sweet Turkish coffee. The diver, Mehmet Aşkin (pronounced Ashkin), played cards at a neighboring table. He never glanced at us. After half an hour I asked our Mehmet when something would happen. He told me to be patient.

Mehmet Aşkin finished his game and approached, flanked by his companions at cards. With neither friendliness nor hostility on his wide, dark face he affirmed that he knew of several wrecks that he would show us the following week, after he had put his business in order so that he could accompany us. For goodwill he then took us several hours away to a wreck Yüksel dived on with Cumhur and identified as Byzantine. Byzantine! Why couldn't Byzantine captains keep their ships afloat? We knew of Byzantine wrecks in Turkey and Cyprus and Italy, and had already excavated one. I was hoping for something from another period.

We left Mehmet Aşkin near his boat, promising to return in a few days, and continued to Marmaris for another guide. We found an elderly diver selling postcards on the street, so crippled by the bends we had to carry him onto the *Kardeshler;* he claimed knowledge of good wrecks.

"It's over there," he said, pointing across a cove, then changed his mind. "No, it's on the other side."

We sailed in circles as the old man became more confused, trying to recall·a familiar landmark. None of our dives produced more than a broken amphora neck. We returned the diver to Marmaris, thanking him for his trouble.

A twenty-two-hour sail away, past Cape Gelidonya, lay two wrecks Don Frey and Yüksel had visited in 1971. As we motored through the night it was impossible to sleep in the fish hold, which served as our cabin, only partially partitioned from the stifling engine room. I crawled from my mattress on the floor, ducking under the four-foot ceiling, and hauled myself up onto the cool of the deck. I found Mehmet and his brother Nihat sitting in the quiet of the bows and joined them.

Two silver ghosts streaked below, taking my mind off the survey. Water phosphoresced in sparkling halos around a pair of dolphins eyeing us curiously by the light of a full moon. They leapt gracefully, first one and then the other, until one almost brushed my arm. I drew back, startled, and saw Nihat aiming a shotgun.

"Don't kill it!"

"They tear up our nets going after fish," he answered. "We lose days mending nets."

Mehmet gently pursuaded his brother, this time, to put the gun back into the cabin. But the moment of magic was lost. The dolphins dived deep and disappeared, leaving me again with thoughts of the survey. I had almost lost hope. Even the wrecks we would see in the morning were not spectacular, Yüksel said, just "worth a visit." At last I fell asleep on the deck. An hour later, when the rattling of anchor chain wakened me, the sun was already in the sky.

From one wreck a carpet of Roman cups, bowls, and huge traylike plates tumbled down a slope of sand and rock. We moved to the other, an undated cargo of tiles a hundred yards away, to make video tapes. Both wrecks were interesting, worth further investigation. But neither lay in sand deep enough to preserve a hull; neither would do for AINA's first excavation.

Cumhur commented on the second site while watching himself on television after his dive:

"I didn't know you were looking for things like that. I know a much bigger heap of tiles near Knidos."

During the 1973 survey we revisited a seventh-century cargo of roof tiles explored by Peter Throckmorton, Mustafa Kapkin, and Honor Frost in 1959.

I asked if he knew of other wrecks. He mentioned two huge jars he had seen seven years before, while diving for sponges.

"There's no wreck there," he added. "Just two huge jars."

The jars were far away. I circled the spot on our chart, but thought no more about them.

The next two wrecks we sought, diving and using sonar in areas described by sponge divers, eluded us. A third I *knew* existed. We'd seen perfect vases from it in the Bozburun coffeehouse. It was said to lie outside the harbor we were now leaving.

I dived with Yüksel and Cumhur, swimming far apart but within sight of one another to cover as much ground as possible. In less than fifteen minutes breathing became difficult. At Yassi Ada I had never run out of air with twin tanks at this depth so quickly, even after heavy work; another minute passed before I realized my tanks were nearly empty. I waved to Yüksel and pulled my reserve lever. Still no air. I rolled onto my back to drain the last sips through the regulator. We were at 150 feet.

As Yüksel hurried to me I drew my forefinger across my throat, the diver's plea for air. He offered me his mouthpiece, but it was of a type I had never used. I had trouble fitting it in place. Water rather than air flooded my mouth. My depth gauge showed we had risen only ten feet. For the first time in hundreds of dives I felt panic. Rationally I realized I was drowning and thought of Ann and my two boys. The thought that I would not see them again made me forget all rules and struggle upward with all my strength. It must have been considerable. I felt myself pulled down by my legs, held forcibly under water by Yüksel. My head was just beneath the surface. He had shot up with me, risking an embolism to prevent my getting one. Now he hugged me with one arm, thrusting his air supply repeatedly into my mouth. I scarcely knew what was happening. Bubbles frothed around my face, blocking my vision.

High waves had prevented Mehmet and back-up diver John Gifford from following our bubbles from the rowboat. We surfaced nearly a hundred yards away and called for help, waiting for a new air supply so we could go back down and decompress with Cumhur, who had now joined us.

We were not finding the wrecks we sought. Worse, after a four-year layoff, I was no longer diving well. I had done better in my first week at Cape Gelidonya.

Even when we picked up Mehmet Aşkin again in Bozburun and sailed back half the distance we had just covered, to find a wreck he described as "big as a house," we had no success. I wondered if we were being purposely led astray; perhaps other divers had talked him out of showing us the secret sources of amphoras they often sold in the illegal antiquities trade. I could read nothing on his broad, impassive face.

He took us to still another site. John Gifford and John Broadwater found nothing. Yüksel and I saw why on the following dive: the seabed resembled the bare expanse left at Yassi Ada after we had excavated the Byzantine wreck; only a few shards remained here from a wreck that had been totally looted.

The next site had been described as "very old, probably Bronze Age," by several sponge divers who had seen large pieces of copper on it. Yüksel, Merih and Cumhur dived to locate it. On the *Kardeshler* we realized they had found something when their separate streams of bubbles converged and rose together from the same place for ten minutes. John Broadwater and John Gifford eagerly donned their rubber suits, ready to follow with cameras and television equipment.

"Don't waste your time," Yüksel said, handing up a fragment of copper hull sheathing as he surfaced. "It's a steamboat."

My ears were stopped by a cold; I couldn't dive. "As long as we're here, do you want to stay for lunch and have a look at the glass Mehmet Aşkin told us about?" I asked Yüksel. "He hasn't dived on it himself, but he says he has heard that it's just over there."

The three Turks dived again that afternoon and returned after half an hour, their hands laden with glass. Fragments of bowls and decanters and raw glass ingots flashed purple and green and yellow as they laid them on the deck.

"There's glass everywhere! You can't fan the sand without cutting your fingers. It's a good one, George, a really good one."

The two Johns dived to the gentle sand-mud slope 110 feet deep. Glass shards and ingots lay scattered in Poseidonia grass over a wide area marked at one end by a mound of half-buried amphoras. Patterned glazed plates and the shapes of the amphoras suggest a late Byzantine date for the wreck, perhaps from the twelfth or thirteenth century A.D., and the thick sand almost surely covers its unique hull.

Mehmet Askin smiled for the first time. He mentioned a cargo of amphoras only yards away, and John Broadwater and John Gifford dressed for diving. But luck had not turned that far in our favor: they found nothing. We returned to Bozburun to drop off our guide and look for another sponge diver who had promised to help us.

"Winter has come," each sailor greeted us in the morning. The first rain of autumn had driven those who slept on *Kardeshler*'s deck scurrying for shelter wherever they could curl up and nap. With two heavy shirts and a ski jacket I shivered in the biting October wind.

We tried to sail to the village near Bozburun where the new guide lived, but towering waves drove us back. We rolled wildly, four tons of equipment lashed to *Kardeshler*'s deck. A high-pressure oxygen or air tank might break loose and crack with the explosive force of dynamite.

But the storm proved a stroke of luck. The team, anxious to continue the survey, grew restless sitting idle in Bozburun's sheltered harbor. We had not planned to return to the glass wreck, but it was now the only place we could reach with safety, running before the wind.

"We just might find that other wreck Mehmet Aşkin told us about," John Gifford suggested.

The storm, growing in intensity, carried us back southward to the glass wreck. We did not know when or how we would be able to return against it. Yüksel and Cumhur searched again for the new site. While they decompressed under the rowboat, I passed a message board down to them. Yüksel drew the picture of a Classical amphora on it: "Found at 110 feet."

I examined both wrecks in a single dive. The glass wreck was as good as they had said. The Classical or early Hellenistic wreck, from the fourth or third century B.C., was partially looted, but probing indicated that most of it was still covered by deep sand. The two wrecks lie so close together that they can be excavated simultaneously by two teams sharing a camp and diving barge. As at Yassi Ada, two ships had sunk side by side, hundreds of years apart. It was more than we had bargained for. Either wreck would have made the survey a success.

The weather continued to help us. A booming hail storm cleared the air, flattening the waves during the night. We glided over a glassy sea back to the village near Bozburun where the new guide lived. Mehmet headed by foot for the diver's house, half an hour away, while we waited in a vine-covered outdoor teahouse. The owner drew cold water from a whitewashed amphora in which he had mounted a bronze spigot: its shape told us it was from the seventh century B.C., older than any we knew except from the Bronze Age wreck at Cape Gelidonya.

"Keeps it cold as an icebox," he said. "It was netted from the sea about twenty years ago."

We learned it had come from the area we had just left, providing a clue to a third wreck in our new graveyard of ships.

Captain Mehmet trotted down the hill with news that the sponge diver had changed his mind about coming with us. It no longer seemed to matter. Everything was now beautiful, even the rain squall we passed through as we returned to the Byzantine wreck Mehmet Aşkin had showed us the day we met him; I had not dived on it then with Yüksel and wanted to see it myself.

I found it a textbook site, a mound of amphoras in deep sand between 90 and 115 feet deep, so close to land that a diving barge would not be necessary for its excavation. Although Byzantine, it was certainly not of the same century as the Yassi Ada wreck. By studying it, Fred and Dick Steffy would surely learn more about the critical period of transition between ancient and modern shipbuilding methods. I thought of it less contemptuously now that it was no longer our only promising wreck.

We sailed directly to the Knidian Peninsula to see the tiles Cumhur had mentioned. The wreck lay on rock, with no possibility of its hull being preserved, but cargo and galley wares were clearly visi-

Two-handled bowls from an unexcavated cargo of cups, bowls, and lamps near Knidos are dated by their shapes to the first century B.C.

ble, dating it to the first century B.C. Far more exciting was a Hellenistic wreck of the same date, only a hundred yards away, with a cargo of delicate cups, lamps, and bowls, many of them perfectly preserved.

After so many weeks of frustration, I had dived on five wrecks in just two days, four of them—the best preserved—representing four different periods of antiquity.

In Bodrum we awaited word from Washington that would tell us if we could continue. When it arrived the news was mixed: the National Geographic Society had approved a supplemental grant of $2,000, but Dr. Carmichael, who had helped our work so much in the past, had died that week.

The sun was low in the sky as we passed the tiny bay circled on our chart. We didn't plan to stop. But I called Cumhur to the stern and asked him again about what he had seen there.

"Are you sure it isn't a wreck?"

"There's no wreck," he answered. "Just two huge jars on rocks." He described them as having wide, open mouths like ships' water jars.

"They're probably Roman," I said to Yüksel. "Tossed overboard," I guessed. "It's not worth a dive."

We were heading for an entire cargo of ancient wine jars farther along the coast. A sponge diver had described them to Captain Mehmet as being long and thin. The site was still an hour away.

Yüksel looked at the sky.

"It will be nearly dark when we get there."

We had dived at sunset before. We had dived when it was cold and windy and the waves high. But for some reason, this afternoon, the idea of coming up with no sun to warm us, of being still cold and clammy when we ate on the open deck, was especially unappealing.

"Maybe Cumhur's jars are worth a photograph," Yüksel suggested hopefully. "Why don't we dive on them now and go on to the amphora wreck in the morning?"

The little bay had by now fallen astern.

I'd had trouble finding the Yassi Ada wrecks after just a year away from them. Cumhur had seen the jars just once, seven years before.

"Do you think you could find the jars again, Cumhur?"

"Yes."

I made a sudden, irrational decision, based mostly on a desire to finish our dives in daylight. I gave the order to turn back to the bay.

Yüksel and I followed Cumhur into the water. With no landmarks to guide him, but with the uncanny sense of direction I've seen so often among Turkish divers, he darted this way and that over an unbroken field of eel grass thirty feet deep. He swam the zigzag pattern he had once used when tethered to the surface by a hose in his quest for sponges. I could scarcely keep up, and found myself panting into my mouthpiece after fifteen minutes.

The two huge jars Cumhur Ilik led us to. They seem to mark the grave of a ship lost during the Iron Age. Moments after the picture was taken, a large moray eel was seen lurking in the farther jar, just before we reached inside to examine it for possible contents.

Cumhur looked at Yüksel's depth gauge and suddenly headed off in a new direction, down a rocky slope. At a hundred feet, just where the rock met a sandy bottom, I saw a pair of enormous jars lying on their sides, half buried in sand; shards of pottery lay scattered on the rocks above.

I swam to one, ran my hands around its rim, and moved to the other. Before I touched it, Yüksel pulled me away from the ugly moray lurking inside. Then he knelt and wrote on the open palm of one hand with the forefinger of his other: W-R-E-C-K. I nodded vigorous agreement.

"*Aptal* Cumhur," I said, giving him a friendly shove back on *Kardeshler*'s deck. "You really are stupid. No wreck? It's the best wreck we've seen!"

It was old—older than anything we had found. We spent the next day raising the perfect jars: a huge open-mouthed storage jar and a giant mixing bowl. We were unable to date them, but fragments of smaller jars point to the seventh century B.C., the end of the Iron Age, the period when Classical Greek civilization began to rise from the poverty of the Dark Ages which preceded. Archaic Greek, Phoenician, Cypriot? It didn't matter. Whatever its nationality, the wreck's historical importance was certain.

Jubilant, we continued to the wreck that had brought us to this part of the coast. Following instructions Mehmet had received weeks before, Yüksel and I began the search. Directions were direct and simple: "Enter the water at the first cape. The rocks drop straight down to forty meters, where sand begins. Between there and the next small cape is a wreck with long, slim amphoras."

Within ten minutes Yüksel had spotted it, a mound of cigar-shaped wine jars from the first century A.D. Looting had exposed part of a wooden hull, but no serious damage had yet been done to it. The wreck was well worth excavating.

If we had found that ship alone, we would have considered the survey a success. Now it was almost anticlimactic. We had located seventeen sites, with good wrecks from every period of antiquity since the Bronze Age: Iron Age, Classical, Hellenistic, Roman, Byzantine, and Medieval. Years of work and an entire history of seafaring lay before the new institute. Our survey had in two brief weeks turned from a disaster into the most productive ever conducted in the Mediterranean. Our only sadness came from evidence of looting on all but the Iron Age wreck; the greed for souvenirs will

The author and Cumhur examine the "huge jars," a storage jar and a mixing bowl, by the recompression chamber mounted on the deck of the Kardeshler.

soon destroy all evidence of man's maritime past in diving depths.

Back in Bodrum for supplies we awaited the morning with eager anticipation. We had learned of still more wrecks to the north.

But the heavy, humid air carried something telepathic through the night. On the wooden platform that served as a bed in the small room I shared with the two Johns, I woke at 4:30 A.M. Unable to sleep, I boiled coffee and began for the tenth time to total unpaid bills in Bodrum. A day's sail to the north lay two promising wrecks and a sponge diver willing to take us to them; a bit farther away lived a fisherman who offered to show where he had thrown a netted bronze statue back into the water years before. But my figures showed no way to stretch our survey longer. We had money for only a few more days. If we got stuck by bad weather we wouldn't be able to pay the crew. Outside, the sky was threatening. It would not be wise to go on.

John Gifford entered the kitchen before seven. I assumed that he, our most avid diver, would be discouraged by my decision. I suggested we might take the tanks north by jeep and dive without *Kardeshler* or the chamber.

"Why don't we stop while we're ahead?" he said. "We've been lucky. We've had no accidents. We've had a very successful survey. For the good of the institute, let's call it quits."

I was relieved. But how to tell Yüksel? He felt an unswerving duty to find and report as many wrecks as possible to his government. When he came down from his room I talked first of other things, willing to continue, somehow, if it seemed politic. I made my suggestion and he broke into a broad grin:

"I heard you get up about four this morning. I lay there ever since wondering how to tell you not to push any more. I decided to ask if you didn't know anything about geography. Just because we would sail north doesn't mean the south wind wouldn't reach us there. Really, George, we might get caught in Yalikavak for four or five days. Then how would you pay for the boat?

"Now you have reached the same conclusion," he continued, still smiling. "Don't push your luck any more."

John Broadwater was ambivalent. He hoped for good color photographs if one of the wrecks was well preserved, but he would bow to majority decision.

I went to the harbor to break the news to Mehmet, sure that his crew would be sad to lose a few extra days' pay. Mehmet met me on the deck.

"I talked with Nihat last night and we think that it is time to stop," he said. "It's been good till now. Let's end it."

Epilogue

I HAVE tried to give in these pages an accurate account of our part in the development of scientific underwater archaeology. However, space has allowed me to recount only the highlights of many years of work. I wish that it had been possible to give all of the dozens of participants and supporters due credit for their contributions; the omission of names is fortuitous. Some of those mentioned were with us for only a few weeks, but appeared on the scene in time to have played a role in some memorable occurrence. On the other hand, Don Frey, a mainstay of the team during three campaigns, was so involved in the unglamourous task of keeping diving and electronic equipment in good repair that his name scarcely appears; Louis Beauvy, expedition doctor for two summers, was fortunate in not having had a serious diving accident to treat, and is mentioned only in passing; others, close friends and valuable assistants, do not appear at all. And I have not thanked adequately the Turkish Department of Antiquities for allowing and encouraging the work. Thus, to the best of my ability, I present the full cast of those without whom the project could not have succeeded:

1960

STAFF: G.F. Bass, director; Peter Throckmorton, technical director; Joan du Plat Taylor and Ann S. Bass, records and conservation; Frederic Dumas, chief diver; Claude Duthuit and Waldemar Illing, divers; Herb Greer and Peter Dorrell, photographers; Honor Frost, Eric J. Ryan, Yüksel Egdemir, and Terry Ball, artists. Helpful visitors were Mustafa Kapkin, Rasim Diwanli, Nixon Griffis, Roland J. Lacroix, Gernolf Martens, Luis Marden, and John Dereki. Kemal Aras was in charge of boats and local arrangements.

SPONSORS: The University Museum of the University of Pennsylvania, the Institute of Archaeology of London University, the Littauer Foundation, Nixon Griffis, John Huston, the American Philosophical Society, the British Academy and the Craven Fund; with gifts or loans of equipment and supplies by the U.S. Divers Co., La Spirotechnique, the British School in Athens, Bauer Kompressoren, Nikon Company, Polaroid Corporation, Anglo-American Plastics Ltd., CIBA, Shawinigan Resins Corporation, Wellcome Foundation Ltd., Scientific Pharmacals Ltd., and Baskin Sokullu.

TURKISH COMMISSIONERS: Hakki Gültekin and Lütfi Tugrul.

1961

STAFF: G. and A. Bass, Illing, Greer, Duthuit, Ryan, and Aras. New members were Charles Fries, physician; William Wiener, Jr., architect; Susan Womer, artist; Frederick H. van Doorninck, Jr., David I. Owen, and Lubiza Popovic, archaeology students; Robert Goodman, photographer; Laurence T. Joline, diver; J.J. Flori, cinemaphotographer; Jean Naz, mechanic; and N.J. Dixon, conservationist.

SPONSORS: The University Museum, the National Geographic Society, the Catherwood Foundation, the American Philosophical Society, the Littauer Foundation with a grant through Colgate University, Bauer Kompressoren of Munich, the Main Line Diving Club of Philadelphia, and Nixon Griffis.

TURKISH COMMISSIONERS: Enver Bostanci and Hadi Altay, assisted by Yüksel Egdemir.

1962

STAFF: G. and A. Bass, Womer, Ryan, van Doorninck, Owen, Illing, Joline, Duthuit, Flori, Naz, and Aras. New members were Peter Hall, Pat Hall, and Louis Beauvy, physicians; Eric Carlson and Önder Seren, architects; Thomas Abercrombie and Mustafa Kapkin, photographers; Oguz Alpözen and Şeref Alkan, archaeology students; and Jack Sofield, Oktay Ercan, Agnes Beauvy, and André Morel, divers.

SPONSORS: The University Museum, the National Geographic Society, the American Philosophical Society, Nixon Griffis, the Catherwood Foundation, and the Corning Museum of Glass.

TURKISH COMMISSIONERS: Haluk Elbe, assisted by Yüksel Egdemir.

1963

STAFF: G. and A. Bass, van Doorninck, Owen, Ryan, Womer, Alpözen, Joline, Seren, Duthuit, Illing, Griffis. New members were David Leith, physician; students Peter Fries, Ridge Kunzel, Geist Zantzinger, and Kiral Nalbantoglu; Julian Whittlesey and Donald M. Rosencrantz, photogrammetry advisers; Avner Raban and Giora Raz, from Underwater Archaeological Society of Israel. Mehmet Turguttekin was in charge of boats and local arrangements.

SPONSORS: The University Museum, the National Geographic Society, the Catherwood Foundation, Nixon Griffis, the Corning Museum of Glass, and Mr. and Mrs. James P. Magill.

TURKISH COMMISSIONER: Yüksel Egdemir.

1964

STAFF: G. and A. Bass, Owen, van Doorninck, Womer, Ryan, Joline, Rosencrantz, Whittlesey, Beauvy, Alpözen, Seren, Illing, and Turguttekin. New members were Bennett Jones, architect; William Beran, *Asherah* engineer; Rudolf Karius, photogrammetrist; Lloyd P. Wells, *Virazon* captain; Bates Littlehales and Robert Fuller, photographers; Gerald Stern, mechanic; Frank Frost, historian; students Michael L. Katzev, Mark Davies, and Sandy Fleitas; and Jean B. Wells and Susan Owen.

SPONSORS: The University Museum, the National Geographic Society, William Van Alen, the Catherwood Foundation, the Corning Museum of Glass, Nixon Griffis, the National Science Foundation, and the Rockefeller Foundation; the Office of Naval Research provided the *Virazon,* freighted to the Aegean by the Lykes Brothers Steamship Company.

TURKISH COMMISSIONER: Yüksel Egdemir.

1965

STAFF: G. Bass, Joline, Ryan, Alpözen, and Turguttekin. New members were Russell and Ellie Fernald. Helpful visitors were Robert E.L. Love, E.T. Hall, Nixon Griffis, and Macleay E. Lawrie.

SPONSORS: The University Museum, the National Geographic Society, the Corning Museum of Glass, Nixon Griffis, the Explorers Club, the National Science Foundation, the Sarah Mellon Scaife Foundation, and Mrs. J. Lester Parsons.

TURKISH COMMISSIONER: Yüksel Egdemir.

1967

STAFF: G. Bass, Duthuit, S. Womer Katzev and M.L. Katzev, E. Ryan, Kapkin, B. Jones, Rosencrantz, Joline, Alpözen, P. Fries, Ercan, Owen, and Turguttekin. New members were Don Wilson and John Cassils, physicians; Jane Cook, artist; Charles Nicklin, Paul Fardig, and Robert Hodgson, photographers; Matt Kaplan, architect; William Maggs, mechanic; Ann Searight, conservator; Tony Boegeman, Maurice McGehee, Bruce Luyendyk, and Martin Klein, sonar technicians; Belkis Mutlu, Gail Hillard, Birol Kutadgu, Judy Hodgson, Irene Maggs, and Anna McCann, excavators; and archaeology students Frank Bartell, W. Willson Cummer, Orhan Gürman, Jana Hesser, Cynthia Jones, Regnar Kearton, Sanford H. Low, Hugh Mullenbach, Nancy Palmer, Marilyn Rosenberg, Marie Ryan, Kenneth Sams, Stuart Swiny, Ted Worth, and Laina Wylde. Lt. Cmdr. John Ulrich and Andrew Wright were assigned by the Supervisor of Salvage, U.S. Navy, to assist in preparations at Yassi Ada. Also assisting were Sarah Cummer, Crisa Kearton, Susan Owen, Joyce Ryan, Judy Sams, and Jack Sasson.

SPONSORS: The University Museum, the National Geographic Society, the National Science Foundation, Nixon Griffis, the Triopian Foundation for Archaeological Research, and the U.S. Navy (Office of Naval Research, Supervisor of Salvage, Deep Submergence Systems Project, Naval Oceanographic Office, and Naval Research Laboratory).

TURKISH COMMISSIONER: Yüksel Egdemir.

1968

STAFF: Joline, Bartell, Ercan, Turguttekin. G.F. Bass visited.

SPONSORS: The University Museum and the National Geographic Society.

TURKISH COMMISSIONER: Oguz Alpözen.

1969

STAFF: G. and A. Bass, van Doorninck, P. Fries, Joline, Leith, Low, Rosencrantz, Duthuit, E. Ryan, Mutlu, Kapkin, and Turguttekin. New members were John N. Miller, physician; Robert Henry, chief diver; Fletcher Blanchard and John Owen, engineers, assisted by engineering students Warren Riess and Paul Dresser; Donald A. Frey and Jeremy Green, physicists; John Gifford and Ludwig Beckman, geology students; Ellen Herscher, Donald Callender, Jeff Klein, and William McClintock, archaeology students; Carl Semczak, conservator; Gündüz Gölünü and Mary Jane Cotton, artists; and Barbara Leith, B.J. van Doorninck, Yildiz Gölünü, and Nancy Fries, assisting in time-keeping, radio-operating, typing, and other duties.

SPONSORS: The University Museum, the National Geographic Society, the Ford Foundation (for graduate students' expenses), the Haas Community Funds, and the Old Dominion Foundation; the Office of Naval Research continued to lend equipment.

TURKISH COMMISSIONERS: Yüksel Egdemir and Oguz Alpözen.

1971

STAFF: Frey, McClintock, Turguttekin. New members were electrical engineer Palmer Carlin, electrical engineering students Atahan Canbolat and Ahmet Ceranoglu, and Prudy Hill.

SPONSORS: The University Museum, the National Science Foundation, the Ford Foundation (McClintock's expenses), and the Blanche G. Whitecar Foundation.

TURKISH COMMISSIONERS: Oguz Alpözen and Yüksel Egdemir.

1973

STAFF: G. Bass, Rosencrantz, Frey, Gifford, and Turguttekin. New members were John Broadwater, Joseph K. Alexander, Cumhur Ilik, and Merih Karabag.

SPONSORS: The American Institute of Nautical Archaeology, the National Geographic Society, equipment loaned by the University Museum of the University of Pennsylvania, and F. Alex Nason (gift for new chamber).

TURKISH COMMISSIONER: Yüksel Egdemir.

Index

A

Achilles, 12

Adzes, *see* Tools

Aegean maritime monopoly, 58–59

Aerial survey, *see* Photographing sites; Mapping sites; Submarines

Afyon, 87

Agamemnon, 12, 54

Alasia, *see* Cyprus

Alexander, Joseph, 205, 207ff.

Alexander the Great, 20

Alexandretta *ad Issum,* 144

Alpay, Gunay, 21, 46, 77

Alpözen, Oguz, 102, 172, 184, 191

American Institute of Nautical Archaeology, 197–205

American Numismatic Society, 132

American Philosophical Society, 45, 59, 66

American School of Classical Studies, Athens, 12

Amphoras found at sites, 21, 71, 72–73, 75, 81, 132, 141, 145–146, 147, 154, 157ff. 172ff., 182–183, 214, 215, 216, 219

Analyzing material from sites, *see* Interpreting material from sites; Dating finds

Anatolia, 8

Anchors found at sites, 71, 126, 132, 136, 141, 144, 147, 148

Ankara, 17, 47, 67, 76, 86ff., 161, 185

Ankara University, 67

Antalya, 32ff., 42; *see also* Bay of Antalya

Antikythera, 111

Antikythera Youth, 62

Apollo, 62

Arabs, 84

Aras, Captain Kemal, 14, 21–22, 25, 32, 42, 46, 67, 69ff.

Archaeological Institute of America, 12, 66, 204